Marine
Amateur Radio

Selection, Installation, Licensing, and Use

The United States Power Squadrons

INTERNATIONAL MARINE / McGRAW-HILL

Camden, Maine ● New York ● Chicago ● San Francisco ● Lisbon
● London ● Madrid ● Mexico City ● Milan ● New Delhi ●
San Juan ● Seoul ● Singapore ● Sydney ● Toronto

The McGraw·Hill Companies

1 2 3 4 5 6 7 8 9 10 DOC DOC 0 9 8 7 6 5

Library of Congress Cataloging-in-Publication Data
Marine amateur radio : selection, installation, licensing, and use / the United States Power Squadrons.
    p.   cm.
Includes bibliographical references and index.
ISBN 0-07-145629-5 (pbk. : alk. paper)
1. Marine radio stations—Amateurs' manuals. 2. Radio—Installation on ships—Amateurs' manuals. 3. Amateur radio stations. I. United States Power Squadrons.
VK397.M35 2005
384.5'3—dc22   2005012158

Questions regarding the content of this book should be addressed to
International Marine
P.O. Box 220
Camden, ME 04843
www.internationalmarine.com

Questions regarding the ordering of this book should be addressed to
The McGraw-Hill Companies
Customer Service Department
P.O. Box 547
Blacklick, OH 43004
Retail customers: 1-800-262-4729
Bookstores: 1-800-722-4726

Photographs by courtesy USPS/Walter Fields unless otherwise noted.
Chapter-opening photo by Index Stock Imagery.
Illustrations by Jim Sollers unless otherwise noted.

Contents

Contents

Acknowledgments

As a dedicated recreational boater and avid amateur radio operator, it seemed natural to me that there should be a book about marine amateur radio. In discussing my idea with fellow members of the United States Power Squadrons, as well as other ham radio operators, I learned that there were many bits and pieces that discuss this topic, but no one specific book. There was no single resource for a recreational boater who wished to become a ham, or a ham who wished to become a recreational boater. It is my hope that this book will serve that purpose and provide the necessary information to marry these two wonderful hobbies.

I would like to acknowledge the contributions of some well-informed and experienced navigators who also share with me the magical experience of wireless communication. Past Vice Commander Frank Wedge, SN (AB4UJ/MM) of the United States Power Squadrons was an invaluable source of information and provided the material found in many of the appendixes of this book. Frank is a "live-aboard" recreational boater on his boat anchored in Fort Myers, Florida. Staff Commander Bob Schloeman (WA7MOV) and Staff Commander Don Stark (N3HOW) provided encouragement and advice on the format for this book. Don spent many hours reviewing the manuscript and offered valuable suggestions for improvement. Many members of the Electro-Mechanical Systems Committee of the United States Power Squadrons also provided information and suggestions that contributed greatly in moving this book forward.

Information on Winlink 2000 and the radio Internet e-mail technology came directly from Winlink 2000 system administrator Steve Waterman (K3CJX). Steve is a true pioneer who opened an area of wireless communication totally unknown before he and other dedicated members of the Winlink team implemented the most sophisticated wireless HF e-mail system in the world.

This book would not have been possible without the assistance of Maty Weinberg at the headquarters of the American Radio Relay League (ARRL). Maty spent innumerable hours researching the files at HQ ARRL for many of the graphics found in this book. Dennis Motshenbacher (K7BV), also of HQ ARRL, provided much support as well as offered some of the staff at HQ ARRL to review the manuscript for technical accuracy. Their comments and suggestions are greatly appreciated.

I would like to also acknowledge a number of companies that provided both supporting information and graphics for use in this book. Among them are ICOM America, Alinco, Yaesu, Kenwood, Specialized Communications Systems (SCS), and Shakespeare Marine.

73
Walt Fields (W4WCF)
United States Power Squadrons

Amateur Radio and Recreational Boats

Most recreational boaters know the advantages of having a marine radio aboard their boats. For example, with a marine VHF radio, you can contact the U.S. Coast Guard in times of emergency, access the NOAA weather broadcasts, and talk with boaters in the immediate vicinity. However, indulging in extended conversations on a marine VHF radio is illegal. Marine frequencies are shared with commercial shipping, recreational boaters, and marine authorities, such as the U.S. Coast Guard and local police departments. Therefore, the contacts made on these frequencies must be concise and pertain either to emergencies or issues related to safety, navigation concerns, or your vessel's needs.

Amateur radio, on the other hand, has fewer restrictions. True, ham radio communications cannot be commercially oriented. But, as long as you're not selling fish or hawking cola, you can talk as freely as you like. The only other limitations on ham radio usage are based on licensing and types of equipment. (In Chapter 3, we'll cover the classes of operator licenses, their requirements, and their privileges. And in Chapter 5, we'll look at the electromagnetic frequency spectrum and how the various amateur radio bands are assigned within that spectrum.)

Ham radio, as amateur radio is sometimes called, is perfect for those who wish to establish contacts with people in local or distant cities and towns, on the water, or even around the world.

Advantages of Amateur Radio

While no one would advocate replacing a marine radio with an amateur radio, ham radio can, and most definitely does, serve a useful purpose for the recreational boater. Let's explore some of its advantages.

To start with, ham radio has a wide range of frequencies and bands on which to operate, which means that frequencies are always available. Specific amateur radio nets have been established to handle any messages a marine amateur operator may send. A net is a group of hams who meet on a particular frequency at a particular time to transmit messages or to discuss a special interest shared by the group. Net schedules are posted on the American Radio Relay League's (ARRL) website and included in the ARRL Net Directory publication. Marine nets have access to the ARRL National Traffic System, which can deliver messages to practically any part of the United States. (A partial list of amateur marine nets and their times of operation is included in Appendix I.) For example, if you are in the middle of the Pacific Ocean, you can use one of the listed marine amateur radio nets to send a message to someone in the United States—all for free. (See Chapters 4 and 7 for more information on radio nets.) Amateur radio operators have also established repeater stations throughout the United States, which have the capability of receiving transmissions and repeating them with greater signal strength over a much wider area. They may also be linked to other repeaters, thus extending the coverage area. Many repeater stations are located along or near the inland and coastal waters of the United States. As a marine ham radio operator, you can access repeater stations to pass messages, request assistance, or even use the local telephone service as you cruise along. (Appendix J offers a partial list of available repeater stations and frequency bands along coastal areas of the United States.)

Another advantage of ham radio is that some of the ancillary equipment used by marine radio can be shared with amateur radio equipment. For example, most antenna tuners used by marine single sideband (SSB) can also be used for amateur radio HF operation. And on most boats, the same antenna can serve both HF operations. All you need is a switching component to change the antenna tuner and antenna from marine SSB to amateur radio HF. Since the marine VHF band lies in the 2-meter frequency range, it is also possible to use the marine VHF antenna for amateur radio 2-meter operation (although most amateur radio operators prefer to use the built-in antenna that comes with the 2-meter handi-talkie). (See Chapter 5 for more on antennas and antenna tuners.)

With the right equipment, you can also use amateur radio to send and receive e-mail via the Internet, again for free. This is particularly useful to offshore boaters who need to stay in touch with the mainland. (Chapter 7 covers this capability and the necessary equipment in detail.)

Perhaps the most compelling reason to become a ham radio operator is, well, it's fun! Amateur radio is a great way to make new friends and expand your knowledge of the world. Amateur radio is a never-ending journey. There is always something new to explore and contacts to be made. You don't need a plane ticket or a passport. Amateur radio takes you there—it truly knows no boundaries.

The Amateur Radio Service

The Federal Communications Commission (FCC) categorizes the various communications disciplines it regulates into *services*. The FCC defines amateur radio as a "voluntary, noncommercial radio service used by qualified persons of any age who are interested in radio technique with a personal aim and without pecuniary interest." This is just another way of saying that amateur radio is a hobby. But that designation shouldn't take anything away from its prestige. For one thing, ham radio is a *scientific* hobby; it's a means of gaining personal skill in the fascinating art and science of electronics, and an opportunity to communicate worldwide with fellow amateur radio operators.

Unlike the broadcasting service—which serves a public audience—amateur radio is used mainly for two-way private communications between individuals. And, unlike common-carrier services such as wireless cellular telephones which provide communication services for hire, amateur radio does not involve service fees.

The History of Amateur Radio

The birth of wireless communication was an exciting event, starting with Heinrich Hertz's discovery of radio waves in 1888 and followed by Guglielmo Marconi's first radio wave transmission in 1894. Imagine talking to someone without wires and poles. Radio must have seemed like magic. Marconi's spark-gap transmitter proved that messages could be sent by wireless means, and it wasn't long before enthusiastic private citizens set about learning how to build their own "spark-gap" transmitters.

So began amateur radio. Radio was an exciting new science, and amateur radio operators were some of its earliest pioneers.

By 1912 numerous commercial and government radio stations and hundreds of amateur operators had sprung up across the United States. To prevent interference between the various groups, regulations were developed by the U.S. Congress, establishing laws, licenses, and frequency allocations.

At first, most amateur transmissions were confined to local areas, but soon amateur radio operators learned how to increase their transmission range, making two-way contacts at 500 miles and occasionally up to 1,000 miles away. Longer-distance messages

Spark-gap transmitter used by Guglielmo Marconi.

had to be relayed from one amateur station to another, and as a result, relaying was honed to a fine art.

It wasn't long, however, before U.S. amateurs began to wonder if there were amateurs in other countries, and thoughts turned toward crossing the Atlantic with wireless radio communication.

World War I

In 1914, Hiram Percy Maxim, famous inventor and designer of the Columbia electric automobile, formed the American Radio Relay League (ARRL)—an organization that was dedicated to the development of amateur shortwave experimentation and operation. With the birth of ARRL, amateur radio was beginning to come into its own. There were over 6,000 U.S. amateurs when the United States entered World War I in 1917, and our Government called many of them into service and relied heavily on their skills. The war, however, also sounded a death knell for amateur radio on the home front when private radio transmissions were banned by the U.S. Government in an effort to prevent interference with military and federal government communications.

After World War I, the ban continued, and amateur radio almost came to an end. However, Hiram Maxim and members of the ARRL pursued Congress until the ban was finally lifted in 1919. The result was an immediate rush of amateurs getting back on the air. In addition, amateur radio really took off due to the availability of surplus government equipment and the new technologies that had been developed during the war years, such as the vacuum tube. Used for both reception and transmission, the vacuum tube increased the contact range between amateurs to 1,000, then 1,500, and then 2,000 miles. As the distances grew, dreams of transatlantic contacts were once again kindled.

Going Transcontinental

In 1921, ARRL sent expert amateur-radio operator Paul Godley to Europe with state-of-the-art radio equipment in tow. While there, Godley tuned to thirty U.S. amateur stations. In 1922, the ARRL conducted more transatlantic tests, and European amateurs heard and logged 315 U.S. amateur stations. Two-way contact, however, was yet to be accomplished.

From its inception, U.S. amateur operations had been stranded on the long wavelength of 200 meters. In time, some amateurs began to wonder about the shorter wavelengths below 200 meters. Knowledgeable engineers of the day thought those shorter wavelengths were worthless, but the same had been said about 200 meters as well. So in 1923, ARRL sponsored a series of tests on wavelengths from 200 meters down to 90 meters. The tests were highly successful, and the amateur world found that as the frequencies were raised and the wavelengths shortened, the contact range increased. In November 1923, two American amateurs made contact with an amateur in France and maintained the contact for over two hours. All three stations were on 110 meters. Additional amateur stations began operating on 100 meters and found they could easily make two-way contact with amateurs in Europe. Amateurs started to leave the 200-meter band for the higher frequencies, and the "shortwave era" began.

Once U.S. amateurs discovered the usefulness of higher frequencies, dozens of commercial companies flocked to the 100-meter region. Chaos was imminent until the first of a series of national and international conferences was held to regulate and partition various bands of frequencies for the different services. Representatives from the ARRL very wisely requested and obtained amateur bands at 80, 40, 20, 10, and 5 meters. These bands were considered worthless by the other services; therefore, no one objected to turning these frequencies over to the amateurs. Once again the American amateurs proved to the world the value of experimentation. Operation on 80 meters was so successful that 40 meters was given a try, and two-way contact with Australia, New Zealand, and South Africa became commonplace. The dream of U.S. amateurs for worldwide communications had become a reality.

Amateur Radio Today

From its very beginning at the turn of the 20th Century, amateur radio has continued its spirit of adventure and experimentation, and the world of communications has benefited from its many discoveries. Along the way, ham radio has grown to become the grand and glorious hobby that it is today.

In the 21st Century, ham radio operators continue to communicate with other hams in the next town, on other continents, and even in orbiting space stations. The use of Morse code (CW) has persisted through the years, and computers using digital wireless techniques have been added to the mix. And hams continue to make important contributions. Many hams have helped save lives by providing communications in times of natural disasters and other emergencies. Some hams have set up networks to pass information back and forth between mariners at sea and their friends and family on land, some establish lasting friendships with people they talk to in other countries, and some just like to experiment by turning a handful of electronic parts into a useful device that becomes a permanent part of their "radio shack." Amateur radio really is more than a hobby—it's an adventure.

The Amateur Radio License

The Federal Communications Commission was established by Congress with the Communications Act of 1934. The goal was to set up an independent executive agency of the U.S. Government with the authority to regulate interstate and foreign communications in the public's interest. All communications services in the United States, whether wire or wireless, come under its jurisdiction. The FCC is empowered to grant, revoke, renew, and modify broadcasting licenses.

The Amateur Radio Service licensing requirements are determined by the FCC, and amateur radio operators receive their license and unique call sign from the FCC once they meet those requirements. The FCC has established several classes of amateur radio licenses based on technical proficiency. All classes of ham operators must pass a written test, and some classes also require knowledge of Morse code.

A Bit of History

Prior to 1951, the FCC had three classes of amateur license: Class A, Class B, and Class C. In 1951, a major change was made to licensing requirements: Novice, Technician, General, Advanced, and Amateur Extra replaced the A, B, and C class designations. Class A became the Advanced Class, and Classes B and C became General Class. The Novice and Technician Classes were new license classes established to provide entry level licenses. The

Amateur Extra Class was the highest level of license and gave the holder extended privileges of operation. Morse code requirements for each class were 5 words per minute (wpm) for Novice; 13 wpm for General and Advanced; and a challenging 20 wpm for Extra. The Technician Class had no Morse code requirement, but the knowledge requirement increased from entry-level electronics and FCC rules to complex technical subjects.

Then in 1991, the FCC created a new entry-level class. If a holder of the Technician license class completed the Novice Morse code proficiency requirement, he or she was awarded Technician Plus, a sixth class of license.

Current Licensing

On April 15, 2000, the FCC issued new licensing regulations, reducing the number of amateur radio licenses back down to three classes: Technician, General, and Amateur Extra. The new regulations provided a grandfather clause for license holders of those classes no longer being granted.

TECHNICIAN CLASS

The current Technician Class has no Morse code requirement, but it does require an applicant to pass a written examination consisting of 35 multiple-choice questions. The subject matter of the exam is taken from ten categories dealing with the FCC rules and regulations and amateur radio operation. The entire database of test questions along with the correct answers are available for study in the current Technician Class License manual published by the ARRL and the No-Code Technician manual published by Gordon West Publications (see Appendix A). The Technician Class license permits operation starting at 50 MHz (6 meters) and bands higher in frequency.

GENERAL CLASS

To receive the General Class license, an applicant must demonstrate proficiency in the International Morse Code (5 wpm), as well as pass the technical exams for both the Technician and the General Classes. Holders of a Technician Class license need only pass the Morse code test and the General Class license exam.

The General Class examination consists of 35 multiple-choice questions taken from a pool of over 350 questions. The entire database of test questions along with the correct answers are available for study in the General Class license manuals published by ARRL and Gordon West Publications (see Appendix A). The subject matter of this examination is taken from the same ten categories as the Technician exam; however, applicants need a more comprehensive knowledge of the subject matter in each category. The General Class license gives the holder access to all amateur frequency bands with all modes of operation and power levels. This includes 160, 80, 60, 40, 30, 20, 17, 15, 12, and 10 meters, as well as all the higher frequency bands allocated to the Technician Class. Licensees of the General Class have just one restriction: they cannot use the additional amateur frequencies reserved for the Extra Class (see below).

AMATEUR EXTRA CLASS

The Amateur Extra Class requires an applicant to know Morse code at 5 wpm and pass the technical exams for the Technician, General, and Extra Classes. The Amateur Extra Class also requires considerable additional study, as the database of technical questions for this exam includes 650 questions (from which 50 will randomly appear on the exam).

The questions are taken from the same categories as in the Technician and General Class examination, except Radio Frequency Safety is omitted. Study manuals for the Extra Class license are listed in Appendix A.

Besides the prestige of holding this class of license, there are additional frequency usage benefits that only the Extra Class license holder can use. These include an additional 25 kHz in the 75-meter band, 25 kHz in the 80-meter band, 50 kHz in the 40-meter band, 50 kHz in the 20-meter band, and 50 kHz in the 15-meter band.

The Future

At present, the requirements for the three classes of amateur license are as described above. However, in late January 2004, the ARRL proposed to the FCC a major license restructuring plan that would create a new entry-level class of license called "Novice," and also eliminate the 5 wpm Morse code requirement for all license classes except the Extra Class license. As of this writing, the FCC had not yet acted upon the ARRL's proposal.

Objectives of Amateur Radio

The Amateur Radio Service attracts individuals with a diversity of interests. There are some who are simply interested in the technical side of radio and wish to experiment and build their own equipment. Some wish to use their equipment and skill to provide emergency communications during disasters. And then, there are some who simply wish to use ham radio to communicate and keep in touch with other hams while cruising the nation's waterways. Hams might be doctors, shop keepers, housewives, lawyers, engineers, students, nurses, but they all share a common interest in the fascinating hobby of ham radio. Ham radio is a voluntary, disciplined communications service, guided by five traditional objectives.

1. TO PROVIDE EMERGENCY OR PUBLIC SERVICE COMMUNICATIONS WHEN NORMAL COMMUNICATIONS ARE DISRUPTED OR NONEXISTENT.

Since 1913, amateur radio has been relied upon for communications services during times of natural disaster and emergencies. In thousands of cases, amateur radio has been the only means of outside communication during storms, floods, hurricanes, tornadoes, and earthquakes. Using battery-powered equipment, amateurs have provided the needed communications capability even when the normal electrical power was out of business. Hams work with fire and police departments, the Red Cross, and medical personnel to serve the public in times of emergencies.

Hams have also been the communications link for expeditions in far-flung locales. The first ham to assist with an expedition was Don Mix, amateur call sign 1TS, who took his radio equipment and accompanied Donald MacMillan to the Arctic on the schooner *Bowdoin* in 1923. MacMillan's contributions were so successful that other explorers requested assistance from amateur radio operators. In subsequent years, well over two hundred expeditions made good use of amateur radio.

2. TO ADVANCE THE STATE OF THE ART.

From its very beginning, amateur radio has constantly stayed at the forefront of technical progress. In the early days of radio, it was the amateurs who were willing to venture to the higher frequencies and explore their possibility for long-distance communications. Build-

11

ing one's own radio equipment has always been a favorite activity of the amateur, and such experimentation and ingenuity has often led to new discoveries and techniques that are adopted by military and commercial communications.

Hams were the first to discover and develop the use of computers as wireless communications devices. Hams designed and constructed the first two nongovernment satellites ever placed in orbit, OSCAR I on December 12, 1961, and OSCAR II on June 2, 1962. (OSCAR is an acronym for "Orbital Satellite Carrying Amateur Radio".) Since then, multiple satellites designed, constructed, and used by hams have been placed into orbit. Like the earthbound amateur repeater stations, amateur satellites listen for signals on one frequency and immediately retransmit the information on another. Orbiting hundreds or thousands of kilometers above the earth's surface, the satellite's signals can extend ham communications to considerably greater distances than the very best earthbound stations.

3. TO IMPROVE INDIVIDUAL SKILLS IN RADIO OPERATION.

We've all heard these two sayings: "Practice makes perfect" and "We learn best by doing." Both statements most certainly apply to amateur radio. Operating skills and accuracy in both receiving and transmitting can be developed while handling message traffic, participating in emergency operations, and participating in the various ham radio contests that are regularly scheduled by ARRL. For example, there is a contest called "Islands on the Air" in which hams try to make contact with the most island stations in the Caribbean, Atlantic, and Pacific waters over a given time period. Some hams use their boats to reach specific islands where they set up a station to participate in the contest. Another contest awards operators who've completed at least one contact in each of the 50 states or in 100 or more different countries. All of these events provide ample opportunity for the amateur radio operator to practice and hone individual skills in radio operation.

4. TO PROVIDE A RESERVE POOL OF QUALIFIED RADIO OPERATORS AND TECHNICIANS.

From the days of World War I until today, amateur radio operators have readily answered the call when their skills and talents were needed. Both the military and civil authorities have a deep appreciation of radio amateurs as a source of skilled radio personnel both in time of war and public emergencies. In 1926, the U.S. Armed Forces established the Military Affiliate Radio Service (MARS) for the purpose of using amateur radio operators to transmit communications between members in the armed forces and their families. MARS demonstrated its capability during the 1991 Desert Storm conflict. During this period, MARS members processed thousands of messages between the military personnel on the frontline and their families and friends on the home front. Although MARS usually handles routine message traffic, it can be used to handle official and emergency traffic when needed. In addition, the Amateur Radio Emergency Service (ARES) and the Radio Amateur Civil Emergency Service (RACES) were established to provide emergency radio services during times of need. RACES is managed by the Federal Emergency Management Agency (FEMA) and operates only for civil preparedness and civil emergencies. ARES is sponsored by ARRL and handles many different types of public service activities, such as communications for community parades and sporting events, augmenting the communications capabilities of local police and fire officials in times of emergency, and providing search-and-rescue communications when required by public safety officials.

5. TO PROMOTE INTERNATIONAL GOODWILL.

Amateur radio operators truly are world citizens—their communications are not restricted by political or geographical borders. Hams literally have the privilege of talking to other hams all over the world. Communication with those who speak a different language is possible because English has become the standard language on the ham bands. Many hams develop lasting friendships with those in other countries and regularly meet on specific frequencies. You might even say that hams help bring the world together in friendship. A fellow ham in my local community regularly talks with a friend in Germany that he made through ham radio. They take their families on vacations together in both Europe and the United States. Truly, ham radio brings the world together.

Hams' Varied Interests

From the early days of amateur radio, hams have been assembling and building their own equipment. In the beginning, they were on the cutting edge of a new technology, and in many ways contributed to the growth of that technology. Today amateurs build their own equipment for personal pleasure and satisfaction, using designs published in technical publications, such as QST, the official magazine of the ARRL (see Appendix A).

However, you can be a ham and never build a single piece of equipment. After World War II, surplus military radio equipment was suddenly available at low cost and could be either used directly or easily modified for use in the amateur bands. In addition, there has been a steady increase in commercially built equipment. Today transmitters, receivers, and transceivers are all available specifically for ham radio and in all price ranges.

With this equipment you can participate in and enjoy a wide range of activities. If you want to communicate with other hams who have similar interests, such as gardening, computers, games, boating, and so on, there are nets that meet on the air on a regular schedule. Imagine getting landscape advice from a British gardener, talking about wine with a French winemaker, or discussing traditional navigation techniques with a Polynesian sailor. You can enter distance transmission (DX) contests that involve talking to as many foreign stations as possible within a given time period. I know one ham who sails his 50-foot sailboat in the Caribbean while regularly participating in DX contests. His call sign with the added maritime-mobile suffix*attracts more calls than he can answer. You can also take part in field-day exercises using portable equipment.

And you can operate amateur equipment using different communications modes, thus challenging and improving your radio skills:

- Telegraphy using Morse code (CW)
- Telephony (voice) using amplitude modulation (AM), frequency modulation (FM), or single-sideband modulation (SSB)

---

*An amateur radio license is issued for a specific address. When hams operate their stations away from the license address, the FCC requires that a suffix be added to the station call sign identifying the new operating location. For example, when operating the station in an automobile, hams would add the suffix "mobile" to their call sign. When operating from a boat, hams would add the suffix "maritime mobile" to their call sign. Maritime mobile stations are somewhat rare as opposed to land mobile stations, and usually attract a lot of attention from other hams.

- Radio teletype (RTTY)
- Digital data (computer)
- Image (facsimile and TV)

Indeed, the complete arena of wireless communications is open to amateur radio.

The bottom line is that ham radio is fun and operating ham radio on a boat is twice the fun because it combines two wonderful hobbies. Imagine cruising in the warm waters of the Gulf of Mexico and talking with a fellow ham in Japan, or Ireland, or a sailor on an aircraft carrier in the Indian Ocean. Regardless of what your individual interests might be, ham radio has something to offer.

How to Get an Amateur Radio License

Earning an amateur radio license is more than just an achievement; it's the beginning of a lasting adventure. Anyone, regardless of age or nationality, can apply for and earn an amateur radio license in the United States. The FCC issues all amateur licenses, at no cost to you.

No matter what class of license you go for, Technician, General, or Extra, you'll be required to first pass a written exam that deals with radio theory and the FCC Rules and Regulations for operation of radio equipment. Each class varies in the degree of knowledge required, and each license earned is rewarded with additional privileges in operating frequencies. The higher the license class, the more you must know to pass the exam. At present, license classes above the Technician class also require that you be able to send and receive Morse code at a speed of 5 words per minute.

Most beginners in amateur radio start at the entry level with the Technician Class, but it is possible to start at any of the three levels of license. However, each step in the license class requires that you successfully complete the lower level requirements as well. Therefore, if you wish to start with the General Class license, you must also pass the Technician Class exam. If you wish to start with the Extra Class license, you must pass the Technician and General Class exams.

When you apply for a license, the FCC requires that you obtain a Federal Registration Number (FRN) through its registration system, CORES (Commission Registration System). The FRN is a permanent means of identifying each applicant or license holder and simplifies the licensing process. You can access the online system and obtain additional information on CORES by visiting the FCC website at www.fcc.gov and clicking on the CORES registration link, or you can telephone the FCC at (888) Call-FCC (888-225-5322). There is no charge to register.

The Volunteer Examiner Coordinator Program

The Volunteer Examiner Coordinator (VEC) Program is an FCC program established to administer the U.S. amateur exams. The VEC Program uses hams who hold either a General or Extra Class amateur license to act as examiners. When you are ready to take an exam, you will need to contact a volunteer examiner (VE) in your local area. If you are unable to find one, contact the ARRL at (888) 277-5289 or go to www.arrl.org to find the address of the nearest VE. Appendix H has a partial list of VECs.

The Exams

The first step in obtaining an amateur license is to study. Once you've made the commitment to learn what is needed for a particular license, the rest becomes easy. The ARRL and Gordon West Publications publish study manuals for each class of license. These manuals include all the questions in the exam database along with the answers. (Appendix A contains a listing of other helpful publications and manuals.)

One of the best ways to study for the amateur exam is through group study. There are amateur radio clubs throughout the United States that offer study classes for the three levels of licenses. To find a list of the clubs in your area or state, go to the ARRL website (www.arrl.org). Here you can find a club in several ways: by state, ARRL area, zip code, and name or call sign. Also ask around. With over 600,000 amateurs in the United States, you may have friends who are hams or who know hams and who can direct you to locally offered classes. If not, he or she may take on the job of mentoring you.

Once you have fully prepared, the next step is the exam itself. The ARRL website can also help you find an exam in your area. Be sure to bring two forms of identification: a driver's license, a birth certificate, a military ID card, a passport, or a social security card. For the written exam, the VE team will give you a test booklet, an answer sheet, and scratch paper. Carefully read all the instructions. There is no time limit on taking the exam, so read each question thoroughly to be sure you understand it before answering.

Technician Class Written Exam

The written Technician Class exam (called Element 2) consists of 35 questions covering the 10 categories shown in the accompanying table. The passing score for this exam is 74 percent, which means you may have only 9 incorrect answers out of the 35 questions on the exam.

NUMBER OF EXAM QUESTIONS WITHIN EACH CATEGORY BY LICENSE CLASS

CATEGORY	TECHNICIAN	GENERAL	AMATEUR EXTRA
1. Rules and regulations	9	6	7
2. Operating procedures	5	6	4
3. Radio-wave propagation	3	3	3
4. Amateur radio practice	4	5	5
5. Electrical principles	3	2	9
6. Circuit components	2	1	5
7. Practical circuits	2	1	7
8. Signals and emissions	2	2	5
9. Antennas and feed lines	2	4	5
10. Radio frequency environmental safety	3	5	—

General Class Written Exam

The written General Class exam (Element 3) also consists of 35 questions in the same 10 categories as the Technician Class exam, but each category requires more knowledge of the subject matter (see table). The passing score for the General Class exam is also 74 percent.

Amateur Extra Class Written Exam

The written Amateur Extra Class exam (Element 4) consists of 50 questions taken from an expanded database pool of over 650 questions. The questions are in the same categories as the Technician and General Class exams, except radio frequency safety is omitted (see table). The Element 4 exam contains far more detailed questions on electrical principles, circuit components, practical circuits, signals and emissions, and antennas and feedlines than the General and Technician Class exams. To pass this exam, one will need good practical knowledge of electron theory and the behavior of radio circuit components such as capacitors, inductors, semiconductors, and logic circuits. The passing score for the Amateur Extra Class is 74 percent, which means you must have at least 37 correct answers to pass the exam.

Morse Code Test

At present, both the General and Amateur Extra Classes require you to pass a Morse code test of 5 wpm, which is usually given before the written exams. This test, called Element 1, consists of five minutes of Morse code in the format similar to one side of a normal amateur transmission. You will be given a sheet of paper on which to copy the code as it is sent. You may copy the complete text word for word or simply take notes on the content. At the end of the five-minute transmission, the examiner will provide you with ten questions about the text. Simply fill in the blanks with your answers. To pass, you must correctly answer at least 7 of the 10 questions. Alternatively, if you fail the ten-question exam but have at least one minute of solid copy correct (25 characters in the 5 wpm exam), the examiner can certify that you passed the code exam. Usually a sending test is not required. The entire International Morse Code is included in Appendix B with phonetic spellings.

After the Exam

When you return your answer sheet, test booklet, and scratch paper to the VE, he or she will grade your exam immediately. The passing score is 74 percent. If you passed, the VE will give you a certificate indicating you passed all elements for the class of license applied, and will forward your application along with your exam results to the FCC. The FCC will process your application and issue you a unique radio call sign along with a license certificate. The call sign will identify your amateur radio station when operating on the amateur radio bands.

Vanity Call Signs

The FCC recently instituted a program for vanity call signs, in which licensed amateurs may request special call signs. These special call signs are taken from a block of call signs that are available for issue. A Vanity call sign can only be obtained in exchange for an existing call sign. Vanity call signs usually include alphabetical characters of personal significance, similar to Vanity license plates on cars. The FCC charges a fee for the Vanity call sign, and—depending upon your license class or mailing address—there are some limitations on the types of call signs that may be available to you. Most hams that seek a vanity call sign wish to have their initials, parts of names or hobbies or just a shorter call as the suffix for the call sign. The prefix for all U.S. amateur call signs is either W, K, N, or A followed by a single number character which designates the location in the United States where the license was first issued. Information about the Vanity call sign program may be obtained from the ARRL website at www.arrl.org.

Licenses for Recreational Boaters

Most recreational boaters who are new to amateur radio should first take the Technician Class examination. This class of license allows the holder to operate on all the VHF and higher amateur frequencies. Since most amateur repeater stations are on VHF frequencies, the recreational boater who holds the Technician license, and who frequents U.S. inland and coastal waterways, can have access to these repeaters using inexpensive handheld transceiver equipment. As mentioned in Chapter 1, repeater stations extend the VHF coverage, and some even allow access to local telephone service. The Technician license is a great way to get started with amateur radio and gain operating experience. Once you're feeling comfortable with basic operations, the next step is to move up to the General Class license.

Recreational boaters who frequently boat outside the inland coastal range of the United States will need at least the General

Class license. This class of license allows operation on all the assigned amateur bands, and since the HF frequencies are where all the marine amateur nets operate, access to these nets requires a General license. Also, if access to e-mail is desired while cruising to the Bahamas or any of the other exotic locations available to recreational boaters, a General Class license is needed to use the Winlink program that provides e-mail service to amateur radio operators. (The Winlink program and e-mail service are discussed in Chapter 7.) The HF frequencies not only expand the operating range but also literally open the entire world to marine amateur radio operators.

Amateur Radio Activities

The activities available to the amateur radio operator are very diverse. There is something for everyone. For example, you can participate in contests, join a net, experiment with satellite and image communications, connect your computer to a ham radio and work with digital communications, construct your own ham equipment, or just have relaxing talks with other ham friends.

As a boater or yachtsman, you may only be interested in ham radio to expand your communications capability while off-shore; however, I have included additional activities here to illustrate the many opportunities available to you through your ham radio.

Awards

The most popular awards are called "DX" awards. They're given to hams who make contact with amateur radio operators in foreign countries. The two most popular DX awards are the DXCC (DX Century Club) and the WAC (Worked All Continents). The easier of the two is the WAC award (although it's not all that easy). To receive this award you must make contact with at least one station in

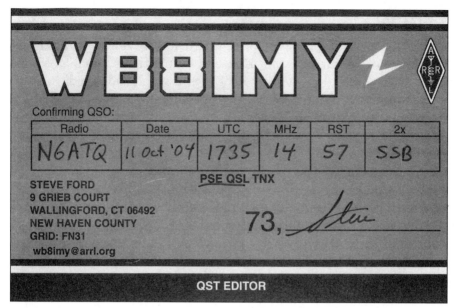

Typical QSL Card used to verify amateur radio contact. (Courtesy ARRL)

each continent (except Antarctica). The WAC award is sponsored by the International Amateur Radio Union (IARU) and is open to all hams worldwide.

Sponsored by the ARRL, the more challenging DX Century Club award is the "premier award in all of Amateur Radio." You earn it by contacting at least one station in 100 or more different countries from the ARRL DXCC List. If you make contact with all of the countries on the list you are recognized on the DXCC Honor Roll! This award is open to hams worldwide.

The proof for both of these awards is a QSL card, which are postcards you receive from your contacts and which serve as a confirmation of communications between two hams.

Another sought-after award is the WAS (Worked All States) award, sponsored by the ARRL. This award is granted to an amateur who has QSL cards from at least one ham operator in each of the 50 U.S. states.

There is a special thrill in achieving any of these awards while operating on the water as a maritime mobile station because a mobile operation experiences power and antenna limitations.

Contests

If you have a competitive spirit, contests provide the thrill and challenge of operating at all modes of competition, such as Morse code or CW, radio teletype or RTTY, and single sideband. In addition, contests provide amateurs with the opportunity of perfecting their operating skills under less than optimum conditions.

Amateurs use a reporting system called the R-S-T reporting system to pass information concerning the quality of the received signal when making contact with one another during contests, and they use the phonetic alphabet to ensure their call signs are clearly received. (See Appendix D for the R-S-T reporting system and Appendix C for the phonetic alphabet.) ARRL sponsors a variety of contests nearly every month. All of these contests are governed by specific rules and regulations that must be followed in order to get credit for participation. They are published on the ARRL website at www.arrl.org/contests. A complete contest calendar for each year is also available. Let's take a brief look at some of the more challenging of these contests.

Field Day

Every year on the fourth full weekend in June, hams all over the United States travel to the forests, hills, campgrounds, parking lots, and other areas to participate in Field Day. The objective of Field Day is to make successful contact with other hams under simulated emergency conditions, such as might happen during a real disaster when commercial power is not available, and stations would have to be set up quickly in field conditions. Field Day really tests the ability of amateur radio to provide emergency communications services when needed to serve the public welfare. It is both challenging and rewarding, in that it gives both the experienced operator and the novice the opportunity to share experiences and participate under simulated emergency conditions. Some amateurs participate in Field Day while aboard their boats.

Sweepstakes

This is probably the most competitive of all the contests because it requires a demanding exchange of contact information between two stations. It normally covers a 30-hour period, of which a station may operate only 24 of the 30 hours. Points are scored for each contact, and point multipliers are given for contacts in each of the 80 ARRL sections of the country. It is not uncommon for some amateurs to earn the WAS award during this contest.

VHF and Microwave Contests

Because VHF and higher frequency transmissions are normally line-of-sight, making contacts on these bands outside of one's local area is extremely challenging. However, when the solar flux index is high, it creates some tropospheric propagation conditions, especially in coastal regions, which in turn create band openings, permitting transmissions and receptions over long distances (see Chapter 6). There are also contests involving earth-moon-earth contacts (EME) on microwave frequencies. EME is a mode of operation where the moon is used as a passive reflector to bounce radio signals back to earth. With a total radio path length of nearly 500,000 miles, this is the ultimate amateur DX. These types of contests are extremely rewarding because they require both great listening skills and operating skills.

Nets

An Amateur Radio Net is a group of hams that meet at a particular time on a specific frequency to exchange information, pass message traffic, and/or perform some public service. Amateur Nets can be broken into three categories: public service, special interest, and message traffic handling.

Public Service Nets

Public Service Nets provide many benefits to the general public as well as to the amateur radio community. Some nets are dedicated to supporting mariners who need information or assistance while cruising or need to pass information to someone either at a land address or another location at sea. Noncommercial messages, such as birthday, anniversary, or personal greetings, may be sent via amateur nets to anywhere in the United States as well as overseas to any countries that have third-party agreements with the United States. (Appendix G provides a list of countries with third-party agreements.)

Special Interest Nets

Special Interest Nets are designed for hams who have a common interest and wish to get together and share experiences and information. Some typical special interest nets are religious groups, computer advocates, and the United States Power Squadrons Net, to name a few. For example, the United States Power Squadrons and Canadian Power Squadron Net meet regularly every Saturday at 1700 Greenwich Mean Time (UTC) on the 20-meter frequency of 14.287 MHz. (Note: UTC is universal coordinated time.)

Message Traffic Nets

Message Traffic Nets are almost as old as the field of amateur radio. In the early days of amateur radio, nets were necessary to communicate over long distances because HF frequencies had not yet been discovered. Today the ARRL National Traffic System oversees most of the existing traffic nets, handling message traffic across the United Sates as well as some overseas locations.

Repeater Nets

Repeater Nets are a special category of nets. In just about every community, hams have established repeater services. Repeater nets usually cover a local area; however, hams have recently been able to link several local area repeaters together to cover several states. Using repeaters, hams with low-power transmissions are able to make contact and pass information throughout their general area, and if a repeater is linked with others, it's possible to make contact out of their individual states. Mariners traveling through coastal waters often make good use of repeaters to make local phone calls or contact friends in the area.

Emergency Communications

Part 97 of the FCC Rules lists emergency communications as one of the purposes of the Amateur Radio Service. The FCC has long recognized amateur radio as one of the most reliable means of medium- and long-distance communication during times of disaster and has called upon hams time and time again to meet those needs. In fact, during the tragic hours of September 11, 2001, when normal telephone service, including the cellular telephone service, was totally disrupted in New York City, hams onboard their boats in New York Harbor provided backup communications for the New York Police and Fire Departments. They used VHF equipment and radio relays for local communications and extended vital communications to other areas of the country using HF radio equipment onboard their boats.

During events such as Field Day, hams demonstrate their ability to set up communications posts wherever needed and to communicate effectively using backup power. Through their membership in ARES and RACES, they provide the means to keep communications flowing in times of civil emergency, as well as lend support to many different kinds of public service activities.

Military Affiliate Radio Service

The Military Affiliate Radio Service (MARS) program is administered by the U.S. Armed Forces and was established for the purpose of providing communications between members serving in the armed forces and their families and friends. There are three branches of the MARS program: Army MARS, Navy MARS, and Air Force MARS. Each branch has its own membership requirements, but all three require that members be a licensed amateur radio operator and at least 18 years old. MARS activities are not conducted on the amateur bands but on frequencies adjacent to the amateur bands. Most activities take place on nets that are scheduled to handle traffic or administrative tasks. MARS operation normally consists of handling routine traffic, but it can be used to handle official and emergency traffic if needed.

Direction Finding

Direction finding or DFing is a fun activity in which hams track down a signal or noise source using portable receivers and directional antennas. One type of DFing is called fox hunt, which is really a game of hide-and-seek. One player becomes the "fox" and hides a low-power transmitter, and the other players try to find it.

Although DFing is a fun activity, it also has a serious side. The skills developed by playing this game have been used many times to track signals from an aircraft's emergency locator transmitter (an emergency transmitter similar to the marine EPIRB). Many lives have been saved by hams using the locator skills they developed through DFing.

Satellite Operations

Amateur radio entered into satellite communications with the launch of OSCAR 1 in 1961. At present, there have been over two dozen amateur radio satellites launched, and at least twelve are still in orbit. Some of these are low-orbit analog satellites that support both voice and CW operations. Working these satellites is similar to normal HF operations, although there is an additional thrill of making contact through space.

Some digital satellites carry packet mailboxes. This is a system where a message is uploaded to a satellite in packet mode and stored in a temporary mailbox onboard the satellite. (See Digital Communications, below.) Days or weeks later a ham—possibly on the other side of the world—can download it.

Other satellites are equipped with video cameras that take pictures of earth and space and make them available for downloading as the satellites pass overhead. Some also carry a system called RUDAK, which allows amateurs to experiment with packet and analog communications as well as crossband FM operation.

Both the American and the Russian space programs welcome amateur radio participation. The American Space Shuttle Program often participated in a program called SAREX (Shuttle Amateur Radio Experiment), which allowed hams to use amateur radio to contact astronauts onboard the shuttles. The Russian MIR space station carried a permanent frequency modulated (FM) and packet station onboard that could sometimes be heard on 2-meter handheld radios. Many of the astronauts themselves are hams and take equipment with them to the orbiting space station, allowing them to make outer-space contact with hams around the world.

Digital Communications

By the end of World War II, RTTY, or radio teletype, became what some consider to be the first digital means of communication (because it was transmitted in groups of dots and dashes). Regardless of where you stand on the issue, it's important to note that carrier-wave (CW) transmissions using Morse code are still found on the

MF and HF bands, even in this digital age. RTTY is still used for casual conversation and for digital contesting.

In 1983, AMTOR (Amateur Teleprinting Over Radio) appeared about the time of personal computers and became the first digital mode to offer error-free text transmission. This system uses a computer processor to maintain a virtually error-free communications link. In this mode of operation, a transmitting station sends three characters then waits for a response from the receiving station. The receiving stations replies with either *ACK* (send the next three characters) or *NAK* (repeat the last three characters). The exchange of ACKs and NAKs ensures there are no missed characters in the text.

In the middle 1980s, PACKET appeared, coincident to and driven by the personal computer. This is an error-correcting mode, which means it is capable of error-free text transmissions. It is called "packet" because data is transmitted in small bursts, or packets, rather than a single, continuous string of characters. However, PACKET needs strong, quiet signals at both ends of the link to function properly. Also, it does not tolerate fading signals, noise, or interference as is found on the HF bands. However, PACKET is the primary digital mode on the VHF bands of 50–54 MHz (6 meters), 144–148 MHz (2 meters), and 219–220 and 222–225 MHz (1.25 meters).

In 1991, PACTOR emerged on the HF scene, combining the best of AMTOR and PACKET. (Even the name is a combination: PACket and amTOR.) It is the most popular error-free mode on the HF bands. PACTOR has special significance to the marine radio operator because it allows you to access the Internet and e-mail using a computer, special modem, and an HF SSB transceiver. Using the PACTOR mode, hams at sea can transmit and receive messages, pictures, weather bulletins, and attachments, all using the wireless amateur radio capability (see Chapter 8).

Other Activities

Other fields of interest for hams include facsimile, slow scan and fast scan television, and QRP operation. In the Q signal code (see Appendix E), QRP means "I am reducing power," and the QRP mode is popular where the equipment is limited to less than 5 watts. Because of the low power limitations, it's quite an accomplishment to attain WAS or WAC using QRP equipment.

Facsimile, slow-scan and fast-scan television are image communications that allow hams to exchange still or moving images. Amateur radio facsimile works much like the old analog fax systems; the difference is that amateurs transmit fax images over the air rather than through the phone lines. Slow-scan television is a narrow bandwidth image mode that transmits images at 8, 16, or 32 seconds per frame rather than the 24 frames per second that is used for full-motion video. Fast-scan television is a full-motion mode similar to commercial television.

The Amateur Radio Station

In assembling or setting up an amateur radio station, I cannot overemphasize the importance of good planning. This is true whether you plan to operate from a mobile station, portable, or from a fixed location. Take the time to think the project all the way through. Determine where and how you will run the feed lines to your antenna(s). Consider your power sources, and make sure you have the proper connectors to adequately and safely terminate power to your equipment. Consider the placement of your radio(s) and all ancillary equipment such as your microphone, speakers, and antenna tuner. If you plan to connect your ham radio to your boat's existing antenna(s) and antenna tuner, consider where you will locate any switching components so that they will be convenient to reach and operate. Having a comfortable and safe layout from which to operate is not just a nice convenience, it's a requirement.

In planning your station layout, consider the type of operating you wish to do, how much you wish to spend, and how much room you have to work with.

Personal safety is also an important factor. High voltages are present in all transmitting equipment, and your ham radio is no exception. Plan your layout such that all electric and transmission lines will be safely routed away from possible contact.

Selecting Equipment

The variety of commercially produced amateur radio equipment available today is staggering. It ranges from small handheld VHF transceivers to dedicated receivers to large transmitters and amplifiers that are capable of operating at the legal power limit of 1,500 watts. What equipment to select will depend upon your budget, the type of operating you wish to do, your electrical power source, and the amount of space available for your station.

Most metropolitan areas have an amateur radio supplier or distributor where you can browse and discuss the advantages and capabilities of different models with knowledgeable sales personnel. The ARRL website offers a directory of amateur radio equipment manufacturers as well as a section for the sale of previously owned equipment at modest prices.

HF Equipment

Because of the space restrictions aboard a boat, most hams who wish to operate on the HF bands select compact transceivers that operate directly from the boat's battery source and are capable of radiating 50 to 100 watts of power. Practically every manufacturer of

The Alinco DX-70 HF transceiver is extremely compact and capable of operation on all the amateur radio HF bands. It provides 100 watts output from a 12 VDC battery power source.

The ICOM IC-718 transceiver can be operated from the boat's 12 VDC power source, and is capable of operating on all the amateur HF bands with 100 watts output.

commercial amateur radio equipment has several models that fit this description. Two transceivers of this type are illustrated here. Both are capable of 100 watts of radiated power, run off a 12-volt battery system, are extremely compact, transmit on all the amateur HF bands, and receive continuously from the AM broadcast band to 30 MHz.

Some hams choose to build their own station equipment. Owning and operating an amateur radio station that you've custom-designed and built can be immensely satisfying.

VHF Equipment

If you're interested in operating the amateur VHF bands, you'll find a large selection of commercial equipment ranging from small handheld transceivers to fixed-mount units that can be easily

A typical handheld 2-meter amateur transceiver can function as a completely self-contained VHF amateur radio station.

installed on a boat and powered by the boat's battery. The accompanying photo shows a typical handheld 2-meter transceiver that operates with a rubber ducky antenna, a self-contained rechargeable battery, and sufficient power to access the many repeater stations located near coastal waterways. As discussed in Chapter 3, operation on the amateur VHF bands only requires the entry-level Technician License.

Assembling the Station

Once you have selected your equipment and the area where you intend to install it, the next task is to assemble and connect your amateur radio station. Most equipment will come with some cables to help you connect the various components. But in some cases, you will have to make your own cables and connectors. Making your own cables allows you to cut the exact length you need for a particular connection, but it can also lead to problems if connectors are not properly assembled. A poor-quality connection can be a source of intermittent problems or radio frequency interference, as well as a potential fire hazard. If you choose to make your own cables, use good quality wire of the proper size, and make sure your connections are solid, both mechanically and electrically. Wires used for power connections to the radio equipment should be at least 12 American wire gauge (AWG) stranded copper wire with marine-grade insulation. The American Boat and Yacht Council (ABYC) recommends thermoplastic-insulated copper conductors. If a cable containing two conductors is used in place of single conductors, it should be type UL 1426BC (Boat Cable).

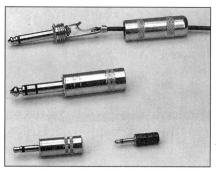

Phone plugs used for audio connections. (Courtesy ARRL)

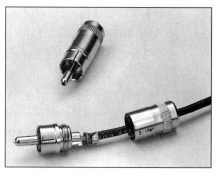

Phono plugs also used for audio connections. (Courtesy ARRL)

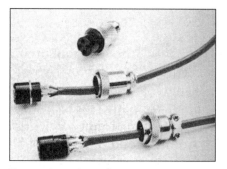

Four-pin microphone connectors. (Courtesy ARRL)

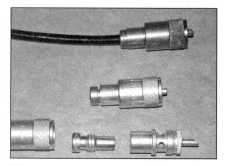

The component parts of a PL-259 RF connector. (Courtesy ARRL)

Let's face it—there are a lot of connectors used in assembling amateur radio equipment. There are audio, power, control, computer, and RF connectors. And in each category there are numerous types that serve different purposes. One good thing about the connectors is that many amateur radio equipment manufacturers stick to a few standard types in each category. Among the audio connectors, the more common types are phone plugs, phono plugs, and 4- or 8-pin microphone connectors.

RF connectors are used to connect the radio to the antenna and antenna tuner (if one is used). The three most common RF connectors are

- PL-259 UHF connector—almost universal for amateur work, used for both HF and VHF RF connections.

- BNC connector—used for low-power VHF amateur applications.
- Type N connector—must be used for high-power VHF work.

Unless you plan on operating high-power VHF, the PL-259 connector is the only RF connector you'll need. The PL-259 connector is available in two types, the solder type and the crimp type. Unless

you have a professional UHF crimping tool, plan on using the solder type. Assembling the PL-259 connector with coax cable can be a little tricky the first time and takes a little patience. Take a look at the accompanying figure. The first step (A) is to remove approximately ¾ inch from the outer jacket, braid, and inner dielectric from the end of the coax cable. This will leave approximately ¾ inch of the center conductor exposed, as shown

Typical BNC RF connector. (Courtesy ARRL)

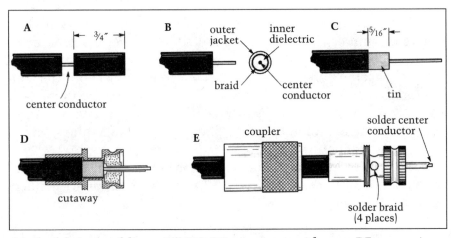

Method for assembling a PL-259 RF connector with coax RF transmission cable. (Courtesy ARRL)

in (B). Next remove approximately ⁵⁄₁₆ inch from the outer jacket leaving approximately ⁵⁄₁₆ inch of the copper braid exposed as shown in (C). Now slip the coupler of the PL-259 connector onto the coax cable and push the body of the connector onto the exposed braid and center conductor, making sure the center conductor slides into center pin on the PL-259 connector as shown in (D). The next part is the tricky part, and requires a steady hand. With a hot soldering iron, solder the center conductor to the center pin, and solder the braid through the four holes of the connector as shown in (E). Have patience.

If you plan on using a computer to access the Internet (see Chapter 8), you will need a 9-pin serial-port connector to plug into the HF modem required for wireless e-mail. Serial-port connectors come in two sizes, the 9-pin and 25-pin connector. The accompanying illustration shows the

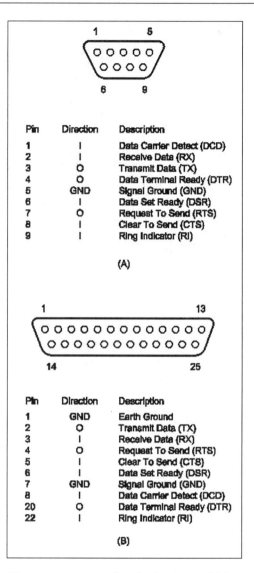

Pin arrangement for the 9-pin and 25-pin RS-232 connectors. (Courtesy ARRL)

pin arrangement of both the 9-pin and 25-pin connector. Some newer notebook computers do not have a serial port, and only have USB connectors. If this is your case, the cable connecting the computer to the HF modem must have a 9-pin serial port connector on one end and a USB connector on the other.

Marine, Mobile, and Portable Amateur Stations

Portable and mobile amateur stations are similar in that they're both established and operated away from a fixed environment. The difference is that the portable station is set up and operated on land, whereas the mobile station is set up and operated in a boat or other vehicle.

There are some basic elements that apply to setting up an amateur radio station—no matter where it's located—as well as some additional constraints that pertain only to mobile or portable operation. The basics include space and location requirements, grounding requirements, adequate electrical power to operate the equipment, and antenna designs. In addition, a mobile or portable station will generally be more vulnerable to harsh environments than a fixed station. These constraints can be considerably more challenging because of the small amount of space normally available for a mobile or portable station: the antenna designs are limited to either a vertical or long wire, the RF ground is more difficult to achieve, and the electrical power is normally limited to a battery source.

Mobile Operation

In most mobile station operations, the electrical power source is the battery system that supports the vehicle. Some larger boats as well as recreational land vehicles may have AC generators that supply alternating current (AC) power directly to the station equipment. Although the term "generator" is generally used, the power source is actually an AC alternator that supplies 120 or more volts AC (VAC) to directly operate the station equipment or to operate the direct current (DC) power supply. If your boat has a generator, the selection of amateur radio equipment that's available to you can be quite extensive.

However, the amateur radio equipment that is most often used in a mobile environment operates directly from a 13.6-volts direct-current (VDC) supply, which is the voltage normally supplied by a boat or land vehicle's battery power source. Today there is a wide range of DC-compatible amateur radio equipment available. If you've selected this type of equipment for your marine amateur radio station, and the current draw for the equipment is more

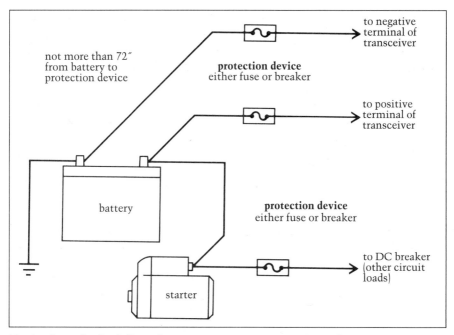

Typical method of directly connecting transmitting radio equipment to a battery power source.

than a few amperes, your best choice is to connect the radio equipment directly to the battery supply, using cables sufficient in size to support the current required. In most cases this will be either number 12 or 10 AWG. It is also recommended to protect the radio equipment by installing fuses in both the positive and negative cables running to the equipment. Good, strong batteries with a sufficient charging system are essential elements to mobile operation. If the battery voltage drops below 12 volts, it may be impossible to maintain proper operation of the mobile station. The accompanying figure shows a typical battery-to-equipment connection with overcurrent protection devices in both the positive and negative cable runs. Note that the maximum allowable length of cable from the battery to the overcurrent protection device is 72 inches.

Maritime Mobile Operation
ANTENNA SYSTEMS FOR RADIO BANDS BELOW VHF
Amateur radio stations aboard boats present even more challenges than operation from a land vehicle. For operation on any of the

amateur radio bands below the VHF bands, the antenna system must have an effective counterpoise. A counterpoise is a system of conductors placed beneath an elevated antenna that serves as an earth ground. Even though your boat may be floating on a sea of saltwater, which is almost a perfect ground, you must still make a ground connection that can function as a counterpoise. The exception would be if your boat is already equipped with some type of grounding conductor that can act as a ground plane or counterpoise to your antenna. When discussing a grounding system it is important to understand the three different types of ground systems that can exist on a boat:

1. DC ground—the negative terminal of the battery or batteries that all of the DC-powered equipment is ultimately tied back to with the negative return wire.

2. Bonding system—system that ties together all metal items that are susceptible to galvanic corrosion; also protects the boat and equipment against lightning damage.

3. Radio frequency (RF) ground for the radio transmitting equipment which serves as the counterpoise for the antenna system.

The first two grounding systems have little relation to the RF system, but all three grounding systems have one single point in common—the boat's engine normally serves as the common grounding point.

Most modern recreational boats have fiberglass hulls, which are basically insulators and will not act as an RF ground or counterpoise. Some recreational boats are manufactured with copper plates or copper wire mesh installed inside the hull or on the outside and bottom of the hull, with through-hull fittings for connecting the plates or wire mesh to the antenna system and radio to make an effective counterpoise. However, this is usually the exception rather than the rule.

RF GROUND SYSTEM

Although the installation of an RF ground system is different for every boat (because of the different hull layouts), the basics are the same. To make a good counterpoise area for the RF ground, you will need at least 100 square feet of metal surface area. (The more surface area available in the RF ground system, the more efficient your antenna will be.) This may seem like an insurmountable challenge, but there are many large metal fixtures onboard the average boat that you can tie together to create the surface area you need. At the frequencies used for radio transmissions, electrical energy does not run through the copper conductor as it does with DC voltages; rather it runs along the surface area. Therefore, using wire to make the counterpoise is not recommended because it does not provide adequate surface area. Copper strap provides more surface area than wire and has less resistance to the RF energy. The following instructions will guide you through the installation process:

1. To start, attach copper strap (approximately 3–4 inches wide) to all the large metal objects on the boat. If the installation of your station includes an antenna tuner—and I highly recommend one—start the RF ground at the antenna tuner by attaching copper strap at its grounding connector and run it to all the large metal objects so that they are all connected with the strap.

2. Next, run the copper strap to the engine block where the other grounding systems are connected.

3. If your boat is a sailboat with a keel, attach the copper strap to the keel by double bolting it to a keel bolt.

4. Also attach copper strap to all metal tanks on the boat—including fuel tanks. (Don't worry, they won't blow up.) This can usually be done using stainless steel hose clamps.

5. Finally, lay as much copper strap as possible within the hull of the boat. This is not an easy task and will take some planning on your part depending upon the configuration of your boat's hull. To hide the strap, some cover it with fiberglass, leaving an area exposed where it can be connected to the antenna tuner.

On powerboats with fiberglass hulls, a ground wire will usually be incorporated into the DC grounding system, which will run

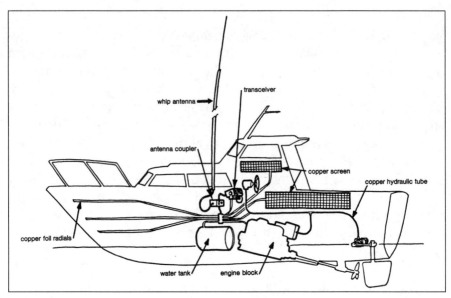

Possible components of a powerboat counterpoise system. Copper strap is used instead of wire to increase the surface area needed for a good RF counterpoise. (Reprinted from The Straightshooter's Guide to Marine Electronics*)*

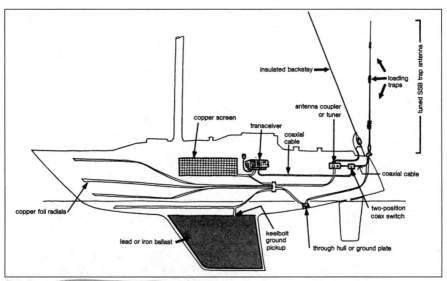

Possible sailboat counterpoise system. Connecting the copper strap to the metal keel as well as other large metal objects will provide ample surface area for a good counterpoise. (Reprinted from The Straightshooter's Guide to Marine Electronics*)*

to most if not all of the metal items described above; however, this will not serve as an effective counterpoise because the wire has little surface area. You'll have to make the connections yourself as described above.

Remember, the more metal surface area available for the RF ground, the better and more effective your antenna system will be. The accompanying figures show a simplified method for installing a counterpoise system on both a sailboat and a powerboat.

ANTENNAS

Antenna space restrictions are another consideration that must be dealt with on most recreational boats. The use of vertical antennas can help solve space restriction problems, but again they must have an effective counterpoise. A standard marine vertical antenna for the HF bands is either 17 or 23 feet in length. (Any antenna shorter than 17 feet will limit the number of HF bands you can access.) The sheer size of a 17- to 23-foot antenna can make mounting it a problem; however, there are special mounts available. Some of these mounts allow a vertical antenna to be lowered when passing under low structures such as bridges and overpasses. The accompanying figure shows a typical marine vertical antenna complete with an antenna mount that can be fastened to the boat's transom or cabin side.

On sailboats, finding space for an antenna isn't a problem. In fact, the backstay or another part of the rigging can *become* your antenna. To use the rigging as an antenna you will need to cut the rigging at two points (at least 23 feet apart) and fit each connection with an insulator that is designed to withstand the tremendous physical stress that sailboat rigging en-

Typical marine vertical antenna suitable for both marine SSB and HF amateur radio. These antennas are typically 17 to 23 feet in length.

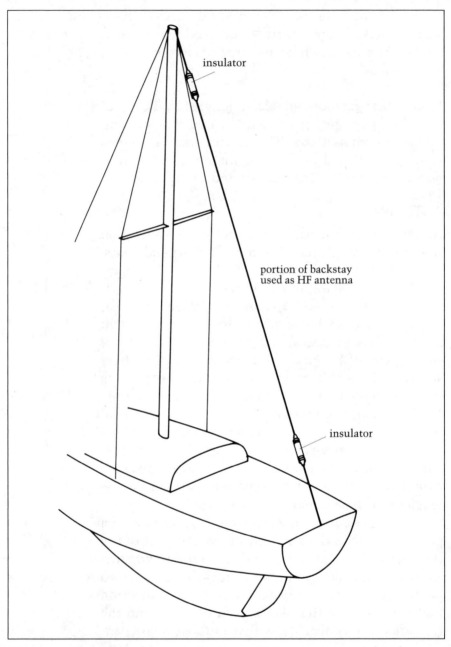

insulator

portion of backstay
used as HF antenna

insulator

Using a sailboat's backstay rigging as an HF antenna. Special isolators must be used to insulate the part of the backstay that serves as the antenna from the rest of the backstay. Because the backstay supports the mast, these isolators must be strong enough to endure high-tensile stress. See Appendix M for a list of suppliers.

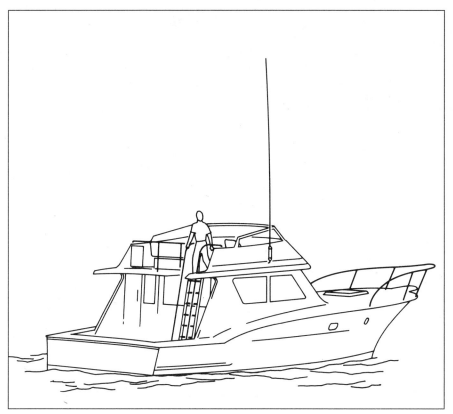

A 17-foot HF antenna mounted on a powerboat pilothouse.

dures (see Appendix M for suppliers of these insulators). Then attach the 23-foot portion of cut rigging to the insulators.

The masts on sailboats can also serve as an effective mount for a vertical antenna; however, since vertical antennas need to be at least 17 feet tall, they can increase the overall height of the mast considerably. On smaller powerboats, your only choice will be a vertical antenna installed either on the transom or on the side of the boat's cabin or radar arch. The accompanying figure shows a typical installation of vertical antennas installed on the side of a boat's cabin.

Keep in mind that RF energy output can be as high as 5,000 volts at very low current and can cause serious RF burns if the antenna is grabbed while the radio is transmitting. If your antenna is installed low on your boat, like on a backstay, you need to provide

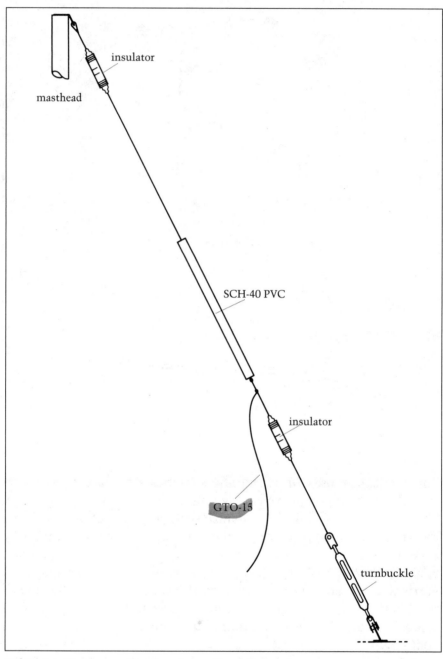

PVC pipe can be used to insulate a backstay antenna to prevent acci-
dental exposure to RF burns. The GTO-15 wire is a special single con-
ductor antenna lead-in wire that can be found at most marine supply
stores. See Appendix M for a list of suppliers.

some type of cover to prevent someone from accidentally touching the antenna. A short piece of inexpensive, schedule 40 PVC pipe does the job quite well (see figure on facing page).

ANTENNA TUNER

HF antenna systems installed on a boat require an antenna tuner. An antenna tuner is an electronic box that changes the electrical length of the antenna to match the output frequency of the radio. This allows you to transmit on different frequencies without physically changing the length or configuration of your antenna. It is an essential part of the overall HF amateur radio station installation.

A typical manual antenna tuner. Note that several controls must be adjusted every time the frequency is changed. (Courtesy MFJ Enterprises, Inc.)

Most antenna tuners designed for amateur use on the HF bands do an effective job matching practically any antenna to the output of the radio, as long as the boat has an effective RF ground or counterpoise.

Antenna tuners come in two varieties—manual and automatic. Manual tuners require that you make adjustments every time you change frequency, while automatic tuners do this task for you. An automatic tuner, although more expensive than a manual tuner, is preferred aboard a boat. The shorter the connection between the tuner and the antenna, the

A typical automatic antenna tuner. Because there are no adjustment controls, the tuner does not need to be within arm's reach of an operator. Instead, it can be placed near or adjacent to the antenna. (Courtesy ICOM America)

more efficient the antenna system will be. Because you don't have to make adjustments to an automatic tuner each time you change frequencies, you can place the tuner near the antenna. However, because a manual tuner requires adjustments, you need to install it close to the radio set, which is usually some distance from the antenna. The accompanying figures show a typical manual antenna tuner and a typical automatic tuner. Note that the automatic tuner, unlike the manual tuner, has no knobs or dials to adjust.

CABLES AND CONNECTIONS

In order to connect your radio to the antenna tuner and antenna, you must use a transmission line suitable for handling RF energy. The transmission line from the radio to the tuner should be coax cable. There is a large family of coax cables that range in size from the small RG 58 and RG 59 coax to half-inch or larger coax cables, such as RG 8U and RG 213. The latter choices are 50-ohm coax cables that are used with radios rated for 50-ohm impedance. They are the preferred coax for boat use.

Use PL-259 RF connectors on the ends of the coax cable to connect to the radio and the tuner. It is possible to buy short lengths of coax with PL-259 connectors already in place; however, most hams prefer to make their own custom-length cables to fit their specific needs.

The connection from the antenna tuner to the antenna is made with a special, single conductor, antenna lead-in wire called GTO-15—a high-voltage wire with a very thick jacket and special insulation material rated at 15,000 volts. GTO-15 can handle the much higher voltages that RF antenna systems develop. Installation instructions follow:

1. Solder one end of the GTO-15 wire to a properly sized ring terminal and attach it to the single threaded output of the antenna tuner.

2. Attach the other end of the GTO-15 wire to the antenna. (If you're using the backstay rigging as the antenna, attach the GTO-15 wire with either a stainless-steel hose clamp or a brass clamp.)

3. Using a waterproof sealing tape such as 3M 2242, tightly wrap both the terminal end at the tuner and

the end attached to the antenna. It is important to keep these connections watertight and dry.

ANTENNA SYSTEMS FOR VHF BANDS

The overall installation for operation on the amateur VHF bands is much simpler than the lower frequencies. You won't need a counterpoise or an antenna tuner for the VHF antenna. In the VHF band, the wavelength of the radiated radio signal is so short—2 meters (6.56 feet) at 150 MHz—that a half-wave antenna of 40 inches is practical. Because the effective length of the antenna is at least one-half wavelength, no ground or counterpoise is necessary. In fact, most handheld VHF transceivers use a special short *rubber ducky* antenna that is directly attached to the transceiver (see photo). These antennas have wire coils wound around a ferrite core that gives the antenna an electrical length approaching a half wavelength of the operating frequency. This type of antenna gives you freedom of mobility; however, it does sacrifice RF efficiency.

THE ENVIRONMENT

Electronic equipment installed on a boat will experience exposure to harsh environmental conditions. This is especially true for boats in a saltwater environment. Therefore, when planning the radio station layout for your boat, be sure to install the radio equipment where it is protected from water spray and excessive moisture. Inspect connections periodically for corrosion, and wipe cables clean from time to time. Remember that your equipment represents not only a monetary investment but also one of safety and enjoyment.

A typical rubber ducky antenna. The BNC connector can quickly and easily be attached to an amateur VHF handheld transceiver.

Land Mobile Operation

Some hams choose radio equipment that can be easily transferred from their boats to their land vehicles. When operated from a car,

Typical vertical antenna with center loading coil.

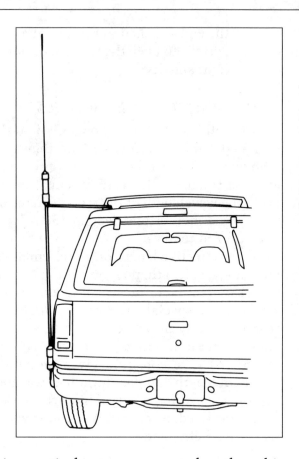

the ideal antenna setup is a vertical antenna mounted on the vehicle. The metal of the body provides an effective counterpoise for the antenna. There are many very good commercial antennas and antenna mounts made especially for land vehicles.

When deciding between constructing or purchasing the ideal mobile antenna, keep the following characteristics in mind:

- The antenna should be structurally stable and upright when mounted on the vehicle.

- Since the antenna will be exposed to the open road, it should be weatherproof.

- If the mobile operation will be on the HF bands, you'll need a long antenna; however, it's not practical to drive around with a 23-foot antenna on your car. One way to solve this is to use a loading coil. A loading coil is a coil of wire wound around a phenolic or fiberglass tube and encased in weatherproof housing. The loading coil is attached to the antenna either at a center point or at the bottom of the antenna. With a loading coil, a shorter, highway-practical length of antenna can be "electrically lengthened" to the output frequency of the ham radio without changing its physical length.

POWER CONNECTORS

The power connections to the radio are basically the same for a car as they are for a boat—in both cases the radio is powered by a battery. Consult the manufacturer's operating and installation instructions to be sure the wires you use are correctly sized to handle the large amount of current that's required when the radio is in a transmit mode. The RF cables used in land mobile operation are usually coax cable. Since the vehicle's metal body serves as the RF counterpoise, the connection from the radio to the antenna can be a single coax cable run, with the center conductor of the cable attached to the antenna, and the outer shield conductor attached to the ground lug of the antenna mount.

Portable Operation

Many newcomers to amateur radio experience the thrill of portable operation during the annual Field Day exercise where they assist in setting up and operating an effective portable radio station. As discussed earlier, the experience gained during this annual event can be extremely useful if ever the need arises in a local community where emergency communications are required.

A portable station, like the mobile station, is far removed from the convenience of a commercial power source, and finding an energy source presents a problem. Most portable amateur radio equipment today can operate directly from a DC battery supply; however, batteries only provide temporary power—eventually, you'll need to recharge them. An AC generator provides a more practical source of power for portable operation.

Antennas are another area where some practical planning is in order. A portable antenna must be lightweight, compact enough to carry, and easy to assemble and erect in the field. If wire antennas are used, they should be cut to length for the intended frequency that will be used prior to taking them into the field for portable work. Trees, buildings, and even telephone poles can sometimes be used as support for these types of antennas. An effective ground is also an essential part of the portable station. In most cases, this can simply be an 8-foot ground rod driven into the earth near the equipment. All ground wires from equipment should terminate securely to the top of the ground rod. (Unlike marine operation, where grounding also requires the construction of a counterpoise system, portable operation gets its counterpoise system from the Earth itself.)

Making Contact

The real enjoyment of ham radio comes from operating our stations. But, if you are new to ham radio, that first time you fire up your rig can be a little bit scary. The many buttons and knobs on the radio combined with the sudden vastness of your reach can be intimidating. Even as you familiarize yourself with the hardware, you might wonder, "What am I going to talk about?" Or, you might have apprehensions about how to proceed in making contact with another ham. After all, unless you are an experienced broadcaster or entertainer, talking into a microphone is a new and sometimes uncomfortable experience.

Operating a Ham Radio

Let's take a look now at a typical HF transceiver that might be used on a recreational boat, and get familiar with the various buttons and knobs that you would use in receiving and transmitting on the ham bands.

The transceiver I have chosen is an ICOM IC-718. It is a compact ham radio that operates on the standard 12-volt DC power found on most boats, and is capable of operation on all the HF ham bands with 100 watts of transmitting power. Take a look at the accompanying drawing of an ICOM IC-718 and follow along as I describe each control and its function. Each control is labeled with a number that corresponds to the description and explanation provided here.

1. **Power.** To turn the transceiver on, momentarily push this switch. To turn the transceiver off, push and hold for 1 second.

2. **Microphone connector.** This radio comes with a standard handheld microphone which would be installed on this connector. You can use optional microphones, but you will need to follow the manufacturer's suggestions to ensure compatibility with the radio.

3. **Headphone jack.** When headphones are plugged into this jack, the internal speaker is muted. Headphones are optional equipment, and almost any can be used so long as they are listed as 8-ohm headphones.

4. **Volume.** The inner ring controls the audio output of the speaker or headphones.

5. **RF gain and squelch control**. The outer ring of this control serves two functions. It functions as the RF gain control from a minimum setting turned all the way to the left to a maximum setting at the 12 o'clock position (midway). It functions as the squelch control from the 12 o'clock position all the way to the right. RF gain controls the RF signal level of received transmissions. Much like on a marine VHF radio, the squelch control mutes the audio output of the receiver.

6. **RIT (receive incremental tuning) control.** Turning the inner ring left or right compensates for communicating stations that are slightly off your receiving frequency. It can shift the receive frequency up to 1.2 kHz without moving the transmit frequency of the radio. It is useful when the station you are communicating with is not right on your frequency.

7. **IF shift function.** The outer ring shifts the IF (intermediate frequency) of the radio and eliminates interference to a received signal.

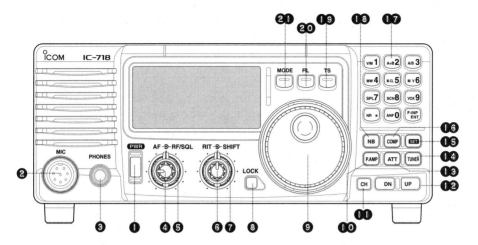

8. **Lock.** If this switch is pushed momentarily, the tuning dial is electronically locked on the selected frequency. To unlock the dial, simply push the switch again.

9. **Main tuning dial.** This is used to select an operating frequency.

10. **Preamp.** When this switch is pushed, the received signal is amplified. It is used to help receive weak signals.

11. **Channel.** This radio has 101 memory channels that can be programmed to allow quick access to often-used frequencies. Pushing this switch allows the operator to select any of the programmed 101 channels by using the up/down keys (shown in Number 12), or program any of the memory channels with a desired frequency using the radio's keypad (Number 17).

12. **Up/down.** These switches have multiple functions. When used with the channel switch, it allows selection of a memory channel. When used as a stand-alone switch, it's used to select between any of the HF ham bands from 160 to 10 meters.

13. **Attenuator.** This is used to prevent very strong nearby signals from distorting your current frequency.

14. **Automatic antenna tuner.** This switch is used to toggle the automatic antenna tuner function on or off. To

55

use this switch an optional automatic antenna tuner must first be connected to the radio. This can be a handy feature for the maritime mobile ham.

15. **Set.** This switch serves two functions. When pushed and held for 1 second, the operator can select multiple values or conditions such as mike gain, RF output power level, and frequency scanning operations. When it is momentarily pushed, it toggles the radio's meter function from an indication of RF power output to an indication of the standing wave ratio (SWR) on the radio's transmission line. SWR is an indication of the amount of RF energy that is being reflected back to the radio while in transmit mode. Too much SWR can damage the radio.

16. **Microphone compressor.** This radio has a built-in low-distortion mike compressor which, when activated with this switch, increases your average talk power in single-sideband mode. This can be especially useful when the receiving station is having difficulty copying your signal.

17. **Keypad.** The keypad is a multifunction device and can be used to select and activate the radio's memory channels, turn the scan function on or off, toggle a noise filter circuit on or off, or select a frequency directly.

18. **Noise blanker.** The noise blanker reduces pulse-type noise such as that generated by gasoline-engine ignition systems. It can be effective when the radio is used on a boat or in an automobile.

19. **Quick tuning.** This switch is used to toggle between 1 Hz and 10 Hz tuning steps when rotating the main tuning dial. The default setting is 1 Hz tuning steps; however, if you wish to tune faster across a band you can use this switch to tune in 10 Hz steps.

20. **Filter.** You can use this switch to toggle between pre-programmed normal, wide, or narrow intermediate frequency filters. This switch can be useful when there are strong stations operating close to your de-

sired frequency. Toggling the filter switch can be helpful in reducing interference.

21. **Mode.** This radio is capable of operating in AM, SSB,
or CW mode. This switch is used to select the preferred mode of operation. When SSB mode is selected
the radio will automatically select lower sideband
(LSB) for frequencies below the 20-meter band, and
upper sideband (USB) for frequencies from 20 meters
and above. If you wish to change this, push and hold
this switch for 1 second. This will allow you to toggle
between LSB and USB.

The functions of the ICOM IC-718 transceiver are typical of
the compact ham radio that most would choose as their first rig.
The placement of the buttons and switches might change with
other radios, but the functions that they control are generally the
same as described here. Regardless of what model radio you choose
as your first rig, my advice is to carefully read through the owner's
manual before even thinking about installing it on your boat. Make
sure you thoroughly understand all the controls and functions before you fire it up and go on the air. Following this advice could
save you a lot of headaches later.

Operating Procedures

Perhaps the best advice for the new ham is to just turn on the radio
and listen. Listen to as many conversations, or QSOs, as you can.
Listen to how other operators conduct their transmissions. Find out
what works for other hams and what doesn't. When you feel comfortable, turn on the transmitter and make your first contact. You'll
be surprised how satisfying that first contact can be.

While you were listening to the bands and observing the ways in
which operators communicate with each other, you probably heard
some hams who didn't exhibit good operating procedures. Ham radio
has a name for these types of operators: they're called *lids*. I'm not exactly sure how the name got started, but I do know that it's deroga-
tory, and no ham wants to be branded a lid. To make sure this doesn't
happen to you, let's take a look at some of the commonsense operating procedures that will keep your call sign in good standing.

Always *listen* before transmitting. If you are initiating a call, make sure the frequency is free and clear before you key the mike button. Even if you don't hear anyone, it's customary to ask if the frequency is in use before making a call. To do so, simply identify your station and ask if the frequency is in use. Say something like: "This is W4WCF. Is this frequency in use?" If no one answers, go ahead and make your call.

Give your call sign as needed. FCC regulations require you to give your call sign at the beginning and end of all communications and at 10-minute intervals in between. If you receive a call from another station, it's customary to respond with their call sign before yours (i.e., "WA7MOV this is W4WCF"). If you wish to call "CQ" to establish a contact, always listen on the frequency first to ensure it is clear, then proceed to call "CQ" three times followed by your call sign (given phonetically) twice, repeat this three times, then say "by and listening." For example, you might say, "CQ, CQ, CQ this is Whiskey four Whiskey Charlie Foxtrot, Whiskey four Whiskey Charlie Foxtrot." Repeat this three times and on the third time say "by and listening." This is good operating procedure and you will be surprised how many return calls it will get you.

Always make sure your signal is clean and within your authorized frequency range. The FCC will not tolerate out-of-band transmissions, and can levy heavy fines and even suspend license privileges for those who stray beyond the frequencies authorized for amateur use. Don't turn your microphone gain up too high, either. Talking louder or turning the mike gain up will only distort your audio. Just speak into the mike with a normal voice. You want to keep your audio clear and crisp.

Don't use CB lingo on the ham bands. There is no place in ham radio for the 10-code system used in business, civil government, and the citizen band service. However, in ham radio, *roger* or *affirmative* means yes, and *wilco* means "I will comply" just as it does on the VHF or CB bands. Beyond that, amateur radio has its own lingo. Ham radio is rooted in Morse code. Because Morse code can be time-intensive, abbreviations were devised to reduce keystrokes. Many of those abbreviations have been passed down through the decades and have migrated to speech. For example, if you wish to establish contact with any amateur radio station you should use the internationally recognized call "CQ," which means calling any station. The Q code system is really used for CW work, but it's OK to use some Q signals for voice operations (see Appendix E), although it's better to use plain language when communicating by voice. And 73 (not 73s) means best regards and is the proper way for hams to conclude their communications.

Know the protocol for using repeaters. Repeater stations can be of great benefit to the recreational boater who cruises in coastal waters. They can be the means of finding marinas, supplies, getting help in an emergency, or making telephone calls (if a repeater station has phone patch capability). If you use ham repeaters for your communications, there are some operating procedures that are unique to them. First, CQ is never used on repeaters. If you wish to make contact with any ham station, first listen to make sure the repeater is not in use, then, after you give your call sign, say "listening." If you wish to announce that you are monitoring on the repeater in case someone wishes to contact you, simply give your call sign and say "monitoring." If you wish to call a specific station, give *their* call sign two times, followed by your own, then say "over." When using a repeater, pause between turn-overs in the conversation in case another station wishes to break in and talk to either party. When using a repeater, never transmit without giving your call sign. A partial list of coastal repeater stations, their operating frequencies, and phone patch capabilities can be found in Appendix J. A complete list of all known repeater stations in the United States can be found in the ARRL *Repeater Directory* (see Appendix A).

Know the protocol for joining a net. If you wish to join a ham net, there are some procedures that are unique to them as well. (You can check net schedules by visiting ARRL's website.) A ham net always has one station designated as the net control station. This station controls all the operations of the net, and all communications should be made through the operator of this station.

1. When the net controller asks for "check-ins," reply by simply giving your call sign. There will probably be several other stations attempting to join the net at the

same time, and the net controller will try to identify as many as possible. If your call is not recognized, be patient. The net controller will continue to ask for check-ins until there are no more responses to his call.

2. At this time, the net controller will call each station in turn for whatever communication they wish to bring to the net. When your turn is announced by the net controller, give the controller's call first, then your own, then pass your communication to the net.

3. If you wish to engage the controller in two-way communication, remember to say "over" at the end of each communication.

4. When you have concluded your communication, give the controller's call sign and then your call sign.

5. If you wish to comment on something another operator has said, give your call sign and say "comment," when the previous operator signs back to net control. Wait for the controller to say "go ahead and comment." Give your call sign and make your comment. When finished, say "back to net control."

6. If the net you wish to join is a traffic net, there are some additional procedures that need to be followed. Traffic is a message specifically for someone by name, generally a third-party message. If you have traffic that needs to be passed when checking into a traffic net, say "with traffic" after you've given your call sign. If you don't have traffic, say "no traffic." Traffic nets can be extremely useful to the maritime mobile ham. Even from the middle of the ocean, traffic nets can be the means to let friends and family know where you are and how things are going. (See Appendix K for a worldwide list of traffic nets and their time of operation.)

These are just some of the standards that all hams should follow. Though they may seem stilted at first, these procedures will soon feel natural.

Remember that courtesy costs very little. Remember also that there are no private conversations on the ham bands. When you communicate on the airways, everything that is said is totally public and can be heard by anyone with the proper equipment. Avoid controversial subjects over the air, and don't give out information of a personal nature that you wouldn't want repeated or detrimentally used.

7

The Electromagnetic Frequency Spectrum and Propagation Conditions

The electromagnetic frequency spectrum is the range of electromagnetic radiation from high-energy levels (with high frequencies and short wavelengths) to low-energy levels (with low frequencies and long wavelengths). Gamma rays are at the high-energy end of the spectrum, so they have the shortest wavelength, and radio waves are at the low-energy end and so have the longest wave length. In between are X rays, ultraviolet, visible light, infrared, and microwaves. We may think that radio waves are completely different from X rays and gamma rays, but they are all fundamentally the same thing—electromagnetic radiation. The part of the electromagnetic spectrum that radio waves occupy is called the radio frequency spectrum.

Frequencies are precise numbers in the electromagnetic spectrum. A group of frequencies is called a band. A band is measured in wavelengths. The unit for frequency was once expressed as "cycles per second." By international agreement, the unit is now designated as *hertz* and abbreviated Hz. Radio frequencies are stated in multiple units of 1,000:

- 1 kilohertz (kHz) = 1,000 hertz
- 1 megahertz (MHz) = 1,000 kHz or 1 million hertz
- 1 gigahertz (GHz) = 1,000 MHz or 1 billion hertz

Wavelengths are expressed in kilometers (km), meters (m), or millimeters (mm).

Radio waves are identified by both a frequency and a wavelength, which means that we can convert frequency to wavelength and vice versa. Since radio waves travel at the speed of light, which is 300,000,000 m or 300,000 km per second, the formulas are:

Wavelength (in meters) = 300/frequency (in MHz)
Frequency (in MHz) = 300/wavelength (in meters)

The accompanying chart of the radio frequency spectrum shows the abbreviation for each band along with its frequency range and free-space wavelength. Radio waves, unlike sound waves, need no supporting medium. This enables radio waves to travel through the vacuum of space and its wavelength is then called free-space wavelength. When radio waves travel through a medium such as wire conductors they are substantially slowed. The speed of a radio wave traveling through wire is about 5 percent slower than through free space.

RADIO FREQUENCY SPECTRUM

DESIGNATION	ABBREVIATION	FREQUENCIES	FREE-SPACE WAVELENGTHS
Very low frequency	VLF	9 kHz–30 kHz	33 km–10 km
Low frequency	LF	30 kHz–300 kHz	10 km–1 km
Medium frequency	MF	300 kHz–3 MHz	1 km–100 m
High frequency	HF	3 MHz–30 MHz	100 m–10 m
Very high frequency	VHF	30 MHz–300 MHz	10 m–1 m
Ultra high frequency	UHF	300 MHz–3 GHz	1 m–100 mm
Super high frequency	SHF	3 GHz–30 GHz	100 mm–10 mm
Extremely high frequency	EHF	30 GHz–300 GHz	10 mm–1 mm

Radio Frequency Management

Under the provisions of the United States Communications Act of 1934, the authority for managing the use of the radio frequency spectrum within the United States is partitioned between the National Telecommunications and Information Administration (NTIA) and the Federal Communications Commission (FCC). The NTIA allocates the frequencies used exclusively by the federal government, and the FCC allocates the frequencies designated for nongovernmental use. Some frequencies are shared by both government and nongovernmental users. Under the provisions of the International Telecommunications Union (ITU) treaty, of which the United States is signatory, the United States is obligated to comply with the spectrum allocations specified in the ITU International Table of Frequency Allocations. In the United States, there are over thirty different radio services that are allocated portions of the RF spectrum in over 450 separate frequency bands. To ensure complete compliance with the frequency allocations assigned to each radio service, the FCC has formulated Rules and Regulations to enforce frequency assignments and procedures. The accompany-

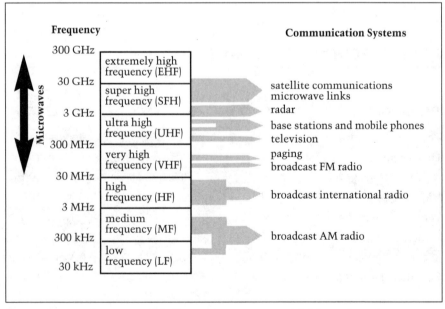

Frequency assignments for the various commercial broadcasting services in the United States.

ing chart shows the frequency assignment of the various commercial broadcast services within the United States.

Amateur Radio Frequencies

The bands allocated for amateur radio use in the United States cover frequencies from 1,800 kHz (160 meters) to 1,300 MHz (23 centimeters). Few radio receivers cover that wide a frequency range, but most amateur radio operators have sets that cover segments of these bands. The following diagram shows the allocated amateur bands and how they are interspersed with other frequency allocations.

Many of the frequencies allocated for marine use are located at frequencies adjacent to those of amateur radio. For the recreational boater this means that antennas and antenna tuners used for marine use can also be used for amateur radio. For example:

- Amateur 2-meter band covers frequencies from 144 MHz to 148 MHz. The marine VHF FM band covers frequencies from 156 to 165 MHz. Transmission characteristics are similar and essentially limited to line-of-sight distances.

- Amateur 160-meter band covers frequencies from 1,800 kHz to 2,000 kHz. The various working frequencies of the 2 MHz marine band are in the 2,000 kHz to 3,000 kHz range. The Marine International Calling and Distress frequency is 2,182 kHz. Both bands are similar, with the maximum range limited

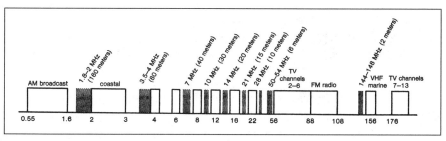

Amateur radio frequency allocations shown interspersed with other broadcasting services. (Reprinted from The Straightshooter's Guide to Marine Electronics*)*

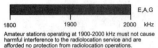

160 METERS

1800 — 1900 — 2000 kHz   E,A,G

Amateur stations operating at 1900-2000 kHz must not cause harmful interference to the radiolocation service and are afforded no protection from radiolocation operations.

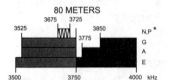

80 METERS

N,P *
G
A
E

3525 · 3675 · 3725 · 3775 · 3850
3500 — 3750 — 4000 kHz

60 METERS

General, Advanced, and Amateur Extra licensees may use the following five channels on a secondary basis with a maximum effective radiated power of 50 W PEP relative to a half wave dipole. Only upper sideband suppressed carrier voice transmissions may be used. The frequencies are 5330.5, 5346.5, 5366.5, 5371.5 and 5403.5 kHz. The occupied bandwidth is limited to 2.8 kHz centered on 5332, 5348, 5368, 5373, and 5405 kHz respectively.

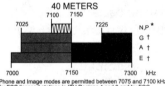

40 METERS

N,P *
G †
A †
E †

7025 · 7100 · 7150 · 7225
7000 — 7150 — 7300 kHz

† Phone and Image modes are permitted between 7075 and 7100 kHz for FCC licensed stations in ITU Regions 1 and 3 and by FCC licensed stations in ITU Region 2 West of 130 degrees West longitude or South of 20 degrees North latitude. See Sections 97.305(c) and 97.307(f)(11). Novice and Technician Plus licensees outside ITU Region 2 may use CW only between 7050 and 7075 kHz. See Section 97.301(e). These exemptions do not apply to stations in the continental US.

30 METERS

E,A,G

10,100 — 10,150 kHz

Maximum power on 30 meters is 200 watts PEP output. Amateurs must avoid interference to the fixed service outside the US.

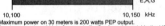

20 METERS

G
A
E

14,025 · 14,150 · 14,175 · 14,225
14,000 — 14,150 — 14,350 kHz

17 METERS

E,A,G

18,068 · 18,110 · 18,168 kHz

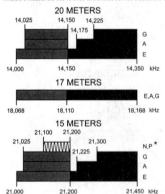

15 METERS

N,P *
G
A
E

21,025 · 21,100 · 21,200 · 21,225 · 21,300
21,000 — 21,200 — 21,450 kHz

June 1, 2003

Novice, Advanced and Technician Plus Allocations

New Novice, Advanced and Technician Plus licenses are no longer being issued, but *existing* Novice, Technician Plus and Advanced class licenses are unchanged. Amateurs can continue to renew these licenses. Technicians who pass the 5 wpm Morse code exam *after* that date have Technician Plus privileges, although their license says Technician. They must retain the 5 wpm Certificate of Successful Completion of Examination (CSCE) as proof. The CSCE is valid indefinitely for operating authorization but is valid only for 365 days for upgrade credit.

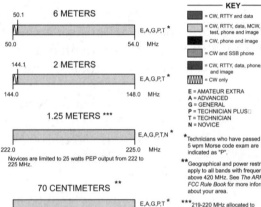

12 METERS

E,A,G

24,890 — 24,930 — 24,990 kHz

10 METERS

N,P *
E,A,G

28,100 · 28,500
28,000 · 28,300 — 29,700 kHz

Novices and Technician Plus Licensees are limited to 200 watts PEP output on 10 meters.

6 METERS

E,A,G,P,T *

50.1
50.0 — 54.0 MHz

2 METERS

E,A,G,P,T *

144.1
144.0 — 148.0 MHz

1.25 METERS ***

E,A,G,P,T,N *

222.0 — 225.0 MHz

Novices are limited to 25 watts PEP output from 222 to 225 MHz.

70 CENTIMETERS **

E,A,G,P,T *

420.0 — 450.0 MHz

33 CENTIMETERS **

E,A,G,P,T *

902.0 — 928.0 MHz

23 CENTIMETERS **

N
E,A,G,P,T *

1270 · 1295
1240 — 1300 MHz

Novices are limited to 5 watts PEP output from 1270 to 1295 MHz.

US AMATEUR POWER LIMITS

At all times, transmitter power should be kept down to that necessary to carry out the desired communications. Power is rated in watts PEP output. Unless otherwise stated, the maximum power output is 1500 W. Power for all license classes is limited to 200 W in the 10,100-10,150 kHz band and in all Novice subbands below 28,100 kHz. Novices and Technicians are restricted to 200 W in the 28,100-28,500 kHz subbands. In addition, Novices are restricted to 25 W in the 222-225 MHz band and 5 W in the 1270-1295 MHz subband.

KEY

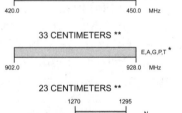

= CW, RTTY and data

= CW, RTTY, data, MCW, test, phone and image

= CW, phone and image

= CW and SSB phone

= CW, RTTY, data, phone, and image

= CW only

E = AMATEUR EXTRA
A = ADVANCED
G = GENERAL
P = TECHNICIAN PLUS
T = TECHNICIAN
N = NOVICE

* Technicians who have passed the 5 wpm Morse code exam are indicated as "P".

** Geographical and power restrictions apply to all bands with frequencies above 420 MHz. See *The ARRL's FCC Rule Book* for more information about your area.

*** 219-220 MHz allocated to amateurs on a secondary basis for fixed digital message forwarding systems only and can be operated by all licensees except Novices.

All licensees except Novices are authorized all modes on the following frequencies:
2300-2310 MHz
2390-2450 MHz
3300-3500 MHz
5650-5925 MHz
10.0-10.5 GHz
24.0-24.25 GHz
47.0-47.2 GHz
75.5-76.0, 77.0-81.0 GHz
119.98-120.02 GHz
142-149 GHz
241-250 GHz
All above 300 GHz

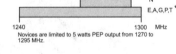

Frequency Chart showing all the authorized amateur bands and the frequencies that can be used by the various amateur license classes. (Courtesy ARRL)

to about 50 miles in the daytime, increasing to approximately 200 miles at dusk.

● Each of the marine SSB bands at 2, 4, 8, 12, 16, and 21 MHz have adjacent amateur bands with similar maximum ranges.

Ham Band Propagation Conditions

Radio waves are propagated—dispersed outward from an antenna—at the speed of light (about 161,800 nautical miles per second or 300,000 km/sec). A portion of the radio energy follows the earth's surface, similar to the way ripples are created by dropping a stone into still water. The portion of the radiated energy traveling in this manner is called *ground wave*. The remainder of the energy radiates from the antenna upward and outward. Some 50 to 200 miles above the surface of the earth is a region known as the ionosphere. The ionosphere consists of rarefied atmospheric gases composed of atoms that have become electrically charged by radiation from the sun. The ionosphere refracts (bends) radio waves moving upward from the earth and returns some of them back to a distant point on the earth. These refracted waves are known as *sky waves*. Depending upon the angles of refraction incidence, a sky wave striking the earth's surface may be reflected back into the ionosphere where it is again refracted back to the earth. When this condition—known as the "skip distance"—occurs, the radio wave will travel a much longer distance.

However, the ionosphere is not a fixed, unchanging refracting medium. In reality, varying densities of ionization create refracting layers above the earth, and greater variations in depth occur between daytime and nighttime hours. This explains the reason why some radio signals in the lower-frequency bands, such as the 160-meter ham band and the 2 MHz marine band, travel greater distances during the nighttime hours than they do in the daytime.

Since the sun is a tremendous source of electromagnetic radiation, communication is influenced by variations in solar radiation during the average 11-year sunspot cycle. The effect of solar storms on the ionosphere can vary considerably from total disruption of HF communications to noisy or weak radio signals. In addition, the amount of refraction in the ionosphere varies with frequency. Radio

67

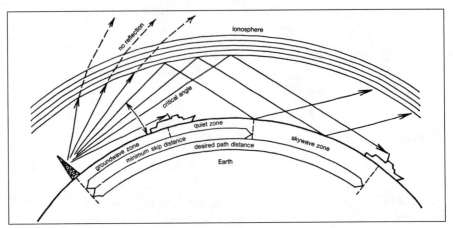

Ground wave and sky wave paths of MF and HF radio transmissions. Sky wave transmission paths greatly increase the distance a radio signal can travel, whereas ground wave signals are limited in distance. (Reprinted from The Straightshooter's Guide to Marine Electronics*)*

waves in the VHF range penetrate the ionosphere with very little to no refraction, while those in the MF and HF ranges rely on sky wave transmissions for long-distance communication. While it's difficult to make precise propagation forecasts in this manual because of the many variables that exist, it is possible to draw some general observations about the characteristics of the frequency bands. The following are some of the more popular ham bands that are considered useful for yachtsmen and their general propagation characteristics.

160-METER BAND

The 160-meter band is in the medium-frequency range and just below the Marine International Calling and Distress frequency of 2,182 kHz. Expect the same conditions to exist on the 160-meter ham band as on that frequency. Daytime distances are generally limited to about 50 miles. Nighttime distances are reliable to 200 miles or more. Atmospheric noise and static crashes can be severe in the summer.

80-METER BAND

Most activity on the 80-meter band occurs from early evening through daybreak. Daytime distance is greatly restricted because sunlight ionization of the ionosphere causes high absorption of radio energy at these frequencies. Daytime distances can be expected to be about 50 miles. Nighttime distances can be 300 to 700 miles, and near-dawn distances of 2,000 miles or more may be possible. Atmospheric noise and static crashes can be severe in the summer.

60-METER BAND

This is the newest band allocated for amateur radio use. It is limited to five channel frequencies at 5330.5, 5346.5, 5366.5, 5371.5, and 5403.5 kHz. Only the upper sideband of the single-sideband mode of operation may be used, with a maximum effective radiated power of 50 watts. The propagation characteristics of this band are very similar to the 80-meter band.

40-METER BAND

This is a popular band for cruising amateurs. Numerous traffic nets operate on both CW and SSB voice. Early morning distances can be 1,500 miles or more, dropping off to about 500 miles at midday. Nighttime range increases substantially and can be 2,000 to 3,000 miles. This band is shared with some foreign broadcast stations that can be heard during evening and nighttime hours.

30-METER BAND

This amateur band is available only for telegraphy (CW). Daytime distances can be 1,000 to 1,500 miles, and nighttime distances are 2,000 to 3,000 miles. Amateurs are limited to 200 watts PEP in this band.

20-METER BAND

The 20-meter band is a long-distance band and very active. Contacts during the day are commonly 2,000 miles and the distance greatly increases shortly after dark. Skip conditions are common, so stations from 50 to 200 miles away may be unheard. The Maritime Mobile Service Net meets on this band at 14,300 kHz, as does the United States Power Squadrons and the Canadian Power and Sail Squadrons Amateur Radio Net at 14,287 kHz. After midnight this band begins to deteriorate until just before dawn, when long-distance contacts can again be made.

17-METER BAND

This is a new, narrow (100 kHz wide) amateur band that offers long-distance capability of 2,000 to 4,000 miles during the daytime. Skip conditions exist and are quite pronounced, with shorter distances of 20 to 300 miles not available. After dark the band deteriorates rapidly.

15-METER BAND

This is another very active band for long-distance contacts but tends to be more erratic and undependable than the 20-meter band. Daytime distances can be 8,000 miles. Again, skip conditions are standard. The band deteriorates to nothing shortly after sundown.

12-METER BAND

The 12-meter band is another new, narrow (100 kHz wide) amateur band that can be a long-distance band. It is more erratic and undependable than the 15-meter band.

10-METER BAND

This band is highly sporadic and undependable; activity depends on the nominal 11-year sunspot activity cycle. The year 2001 was the last peak of activity and long-distance contacts to regional areas several thousand miles away were possible. These conditions change constantly, with some locations fading out and new areas coming in. This band can be dead for long periods of time, with only occasional good propagation conditions.

6-METER BAND

This is the first of the VHF Ham bands. This band used to be a popular local mobile band but has lost popularity because of the 2-meter band. It does have occasional openings for communications to 300 miles or more under ideal conditions; otherwise it is limited to local distances up to 50 miles.

2-METER BAND

The 2-meter VHF band is adjacent to the marine VHF band and is limited to similar propagation conditions. However, amateurs are permitted the full legal power limit of 1,500 watts PEP, while marine VHF stations are limited to 25 watts and encouraged to use 1 watt in harbor operation. Many of the amateur repeater stations are located in this band.

Additional Observations about the VHF Bands

The earth's atmosphere is split up into a variety of different layers, but there are two main layers of interest that influence radio signals. One, of course, is the ionosphere—the region where the refraction of MF and HF radio signals takes place. The phenomenon of refraction, or bending, is what extends radio signals at these frequencies over long distances. The other atmospheric layer of interest is the troposphere. This is the lowest of the layers of the atmosphere and extends from ground level to an altitude of about 10 km. This is the region where all of earth's weather occurs. It is also the region that tends to effect radio signals above 30 MHz, the VHF bands. We normally think of VHF radio signals as being "line of sight"; however, this is not always the case. Certain weather conditions in the troposphere such as a sharp increase in temperature with altitude can create a condition called tropospheric scatter. When this occurs at the highest level of the troposphere, say about 8 to 10 kilometers, a strong VHF radio signal can be scattered and refracted back to earth over a distance of 400 to 800 miles. The same effect can occur when the sun's solar flux index is very high. The solar flux index is a gauge of solar particles and magnetic fields reaching our atmosphere. These particles and fields are carried on what is called the solar wind. Higher index numbers mean more solar wind is reaching our earth. It should be pointed out that tropospheric scatter does not require special operating techniques or equipment. It is a natural occurrence that is totally dependent upon the condition of the troposphere.

Amateur Radio and the Cruising Yachtsman

All of the benefits and advantages of amateur radio we've explored up to now have definite applications for the cruising yachtsman. From anywhere in the world, without subscription or service fees, marine amateur radio can:

- Provide the means for the captain and crew to enjoy personal communication with friends old and new
- Allow access to the local telephone system using the phone patch capability of another ham operator or the auto patch facility of an amateur radio repeater station
- Receive voice weather reports on the HF band and download weather reports from the National Weather Service
- Provide access to Internet e-mail

Coastal Cruising

For coastal cruising near a metropolitan harbor, consider using 2-meter amateur equipment. This is an option available to all classes of amateur radio license holders, including the Technician Class license. The 2-meter band operates on a frequency adjacent to marine VHF and is limited to approximately line-of-sight distances.

The ham radio fraternity has established hundreds of "2-meter repeaters," which are located atop towers, high buildings, and high terrain. These repeaters extend the range of mobile transceivers by as much as 100 miles, allowing the coastal boater to communicate beyond the normal line-of-sight range for VHF operation. Some of the repeaters have an autopatch capability that lets a mobile ham operator place a local personal telephone call (no long-distance or business calls can be made). Such a call is similar to one on the cellular telephone system but at no cost. The autopatch facility uses the standard dial tone multifrequency (DTMF) of the telephone sys-

A WORD OF CAUTION

Amateur radio, like a cell phone, should be *supplemental* communications gear on your boat. VHF marine radio is *a must* while in the coastal waters of the United States because it is your link to the U.S. Coast Guard and with other boats as well. VHF is the first choice for emergency communication. The U.S. Coast Guard monitors Channel 16 on a 24-hour basis and is expert in handling emergency situations. The Coast Guard is currently upgrading their VHF communications capability under the Rescue 21 Program, which will provide emergency communications using digital selective calling on Channel 70. In addition, coastal weather reports from NOAA may be heard continuously on VHF radio.

Some mariners advocate installing long-range marine SSB equipment before amateur gear to take advantage of the 24-hour surveillance conducted by the Coast Guard. High-seas marine operators also monitor the frequencies set aside for public correspondence on a 24-hour basis and are prepared to relay distress messages. Other advantages of marine SSB equipment include pre-tuned channels for marine use, equipment that has been approved by the FCC for the marine environment, and an automatic alarm signal (sent on the distress frequency to attract attention to a distress message).

tem to initiate calls. Most amateur 2-meter transceivers have a keypad similar to that of a cellular telephone that can generate these tones to access the telephone system. Of course, long-distance and business calls should be restricted to the marine operator or cellular phones. See Appendix J for a partial list of coastal 2-meter repeaters. Those with an autopatch capability are so indicated. A repeater directory listing of all repeater stations throughout the United States and Canada is available from the ARRL (see Appendix A).

Because of the very high frequencies of the 2-meter band (144.0–148.0 MHz), handheld amateur transceivers with small, compact antennas may be sufficient to access a repeater network from the water. For more distant communications, the HF amateur bands will provide worldwide communications. The HF bands, however, are not available to the Technician Class license and can only be used by holders of a General, Extra Class, or the grandfathered Advanced Class license.

Using Ham Nets While Cruising

As discussed in Chapter 4, there are amateur marine nets established for the purpose of handling messages from hams afloat. Many of these nets also have members who have a phone patch capability that can be used to pass voice messages directly to a third party over the public telephone system. Distant contacts to speak with a specific person, such as a family member, often involve setting up a prearranged schedule. You can arrange this through the amateur station of a friend or acquaintance or through one of the numerous nets that meet daily or weekly on specific frequencies. Appendix I includes a list of amateur nets that operate at almost any hour of the day. All amateur nets operate with a net control station that has the responsibility of regulating the traffic flow handled by the net. Normally, specific times are posted for stations to call into the net. Those stations with traffic to be passed or with communications requests will indicate this to the net control station when reporting into the net. During this specified time, all net members throughout the country will be monitoring. If conditions are not favorable for the caller to reach the net control station, anyone hearing the signal will help by relaying the caller's message.

One net that is designed for yachtsmen is the Maritime Mobile (M/M) Service Net. The M/M Service Net is a convenient place for yachting hams to meet (14,300 or 14,313 kHz; Monday through Saturday 1700–2300 and 0100–0300 UTC; Sunday 1700–0300 UTC). If you want to contact a specific individual, by prearrangement, you make initial contact on this net, then either move to another frequency to carry on a conversation, pass a message, or if the cooperating ham has a phone patch, connect the radio conversation to a telephone line. (He or she can place local or collect calls to a third party.) Similar arrangements can be made to talk with a physician or hospital in case of a medical emergency. The net control operator can designate a net member to contact the Coast Guard on the telephone and relay a distress message. A phone patch can also arrange for a vessel in distress to be in direct contact with the Coast Guard. A phone patch is an electronic device that interfaces a telephone line with a transceiver. It has built-in connections for a standard

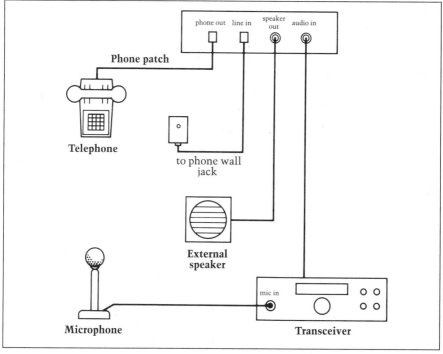

Diagram of a typical phone patch connection to an amateur radio transceiver and public telephone service.

telephone jack, a connection to a telephone, an audio connection from the transceiver, and a connection to a microphone. The figure on the preceding page shows how a phone patch is connected to a transceiver and the public telephone service.

Another such net, also oriented to M/M operation, is the Waterway Radio & Cruising Club that meets daily on 7,268 kHz from 1245 to 1400 UTC. This net accepts itinerary and position reports and gives daily weather reports for coastal, offshore, and Bahamian waters.

The United States Power Squadrons–Canadian Power Squadron Amateur Radio Net meets every Saturday on 14,287 kHz from 1700 to 1800 UTC. Squadron activities, boating news, and radio technical subjects are discussed. Cruising members are encouraged to call in with their traffic, pass position reports, or send messages to family members or friends.

Using Ham Radio While Cruising in Open Waters

Aside from using a net to establish a radio contact, another option is to select an unused frequency and call "CQ," which is the general call that indicates the caller wishes to establish contact with another amateur. Before trying to use a specific amateur band, listen by tuning across the band to see if signals are being received. If not, try another band. When you call CQ, the response is usually on the same frequency as the calling frequency.

A ham operator cruising in international waters uses his own call letters and must operate within his U.S. license restrictions. Upon entering foreign territorial waters, he or she must obtain permission from that country before operating. As getting such permission may take several months, arrangements must be made well in advance of your trip. Frequently, a foreign government will issue new temporary call letters for use in their territorial waters. The ARRL can help with the procedure by providing a contact in the foreign government.

Third-party traffic, as in a phone patch, may be handled only in the United States or between countries with which the United States has third-party agreements. Third-party traffic is generally defined as traffic transmitted over amateur radio that is either to or from a nonamateur. A more complete definition is found in Appendix G along with a list of countries that have third-party agreements with the United States.

Accessing E-Mail Using Ham Radio

One of the great advantages ham radio can bring to the cruising yachtsman is the ability to send and receive e-mail over the Internet using wireless HF radio. With amateur radio, you can use the Internet to keep in touch with family and friends from anywhere in the world, and the ham e-mail service is free. To use this service, you must have at least a General Class License, the necessary amateur radio equipment, a computer, and the required software. Although you cannot surf the Internet with this service, you can send and receive e-mail messages throughout the world.

How the System Works

HF radio e-mail is an indirect connection to the Internet using a special Amateur Radio E-mail Provider. The Amateur Radio E-mail Provider receives your messages via HF radio and stores them on a computer system. At different times of the day, the provider uploads your e-mail traffic into the Internet, and any messages destined for you are downloaded and placed in your mailbox on the provider's computer system. When you connect to the provider via HF radio, any messages in your mailbox are sent to you. Currently the only amateur radio e-mail provider is Winlink 2000 (WL2K). Their website (www.winlink.org) also provides information and operating instructions for using the HF e-mail system.

The stations that make up the worldwide network are called Participating Mail Box Offices (PMBO). Appendix K has a list of PMBOs by country and amateur radio call sign. Your e-mail address is your amateur radio call sign with "@winlink.org" added, for example W4WCF@winlink.org. Because this system is an amateur radio system, no business use is allowed. In the Western Hemisphere, for the most part, there is no restriction on third-party traffic being passed over amateur radio. And since there is no limitation on third-party traffic passed over the Internet, messages passed between PMBOs or a PMBO and the Internet are not restricted. Only when traffic is passed over amateur radio to or from a nonamateur in an area of the world where third-party traffic is not allowed is there a concern (see Appendix G).

WF6F @ WINLINK. ORG

What's Required

To get started using HF radio e-mail, you'll need:

- Amateur radio equipment capable of prolonged transmission periods (with rapid switching from transmit to receive) without overheating
- Computer with a serial port connection
- HF radio modem
- Airmail (client program software)

RADIO EQUIPMENT

Not all amateur radio equipment is capable of the continuous-duty cycle required for HF e-mail; therefore, when selecting equipment for this type of amateur operation, be sure to carefully read the manufacturer's specifications to ensure the transmitter can operate continuously for several minutes without overheating. Icom, Kenwood, and Yaesu all make transceiver equipment that can handle the continuous-duty cycle required for HF e-mail applications.

COMPUTER AND OPERATING SYSTEM

Almost any PC works with HF e-mail; however, it should have at least 256 megabytes of random access memory (RAM) and 100 or more megabytes of free space on the hard drive, and a version of Microsoft Windows operating system. The WL2K system works with Windows 98, ME, 2000, and XP. Note that some PCs generate RF noise that can interfere with your HF radio reception. If this occurs, move the computer away from the radio until the interference subsides.

If you want to use a Macintosh system, you will need to install a Windows emulator program and run the client program software through the Windows emulator. See your computer user's manual for instructions on how to connect your modem and configure the com port.

The software that is needed to connect with Winlink 2000 is called Airmail 3.0 (see below).

MODEM

There are many varieties of radio modems on the market, but to work with HF e-mail, the modem must be able to operate in HF

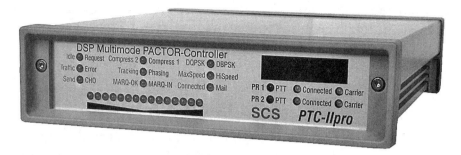

PTC-IIPro PACTOR modem. (Courtesy SCS)

PACTOR mode. The PACTOR technology was developed by a group of amateur radio operators in Germany who later formed a company called Special Communications Systems (SCS) to manufacture the PACTOR modem. At present SCS holds the world patent on the PACTOR modem.

The most recent PACTOR modem on the market is the PTC-IIPro. Older models are available such as the PTC-IIe and PTC-IIex. The model PTC-IIe is no longer being manufactured; however, it is still available as used or reconditioned equipment. Both of the older models can be upgraded to a PTC-IIPro model using a software upgrade available from SCS.

The basic difference between the PTC-IIPro and the older models is the data transfer speed, both transmission and reception. The PTC-IIPro model operates in PACTOR-3 mode, and the older models operate in PACTOR-2 mode. PACTOR-3 mode is about five times faster than PACTOR-2 mode. If you plan to cruise for prolonged periods or in remote areas and wish to download weather files and e-mail attachments, you should use the PTC-IIPro modem. (See Appendix L for a list of authorized SCS PACTOR modem dealers.)

SOFTWARE

Because Winlink uses a computer-to-computer protocol, you need a client program for your computer to talk to a Winlink station. The client program used by the Winlink system is AirMail 3.0, which was written by Jim Corenman, KE6RK, and is available free of charge on Jim's website at www.airmail2000.com, or it can be downloaded free from the Winlink website. If you prefer to have the software on a CD ROM, you can purchase one for a nominal charge of $15.00 from the Winlink system administrator, Steve Waterman, at K4CJX@comcast.net or K4CJX@winlink.org. You may also contact him for additional information on the Amateur Radio HF e-mail system.

Set Up

To set up your e-mail system, connect the computer to the modem and the modem to your HF radio system. To connect the computer and the modem, you need an RS232 cable that has 9-pin female connector on one end and a 9-pin male connector on the other. The 9-pin male connector connects to the serial port on the computer, and the 9-pin female connector connects to the back of the HF modem. The modem connects to the HF radio with an 8-wire DIN Plug. The DIN connection on the modem is standard, but the connection to your HF radio will depend upon the brand of radio you have. Although the DIN plug cable contains eight wires, only four are used for the connection between the modem and the radio. If you cannot purchase a ready-made DIN plug for this connection, you may have to make your own. The accompanying figures show an 8-pin DIN connector and a diagram of the typical computer/modem/transceiver/antenna tuner/antenna connections. Notice that the "audio in" connection on the modem becomes the "audio out" connection on the radio. Also, the "audio out" connection on the modem becomes the "audio in" connection on the radio. The

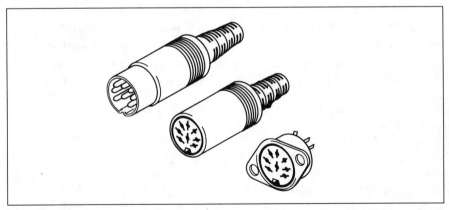

Typical 8-pin DIN connector showing both the male and female pin arrangements.

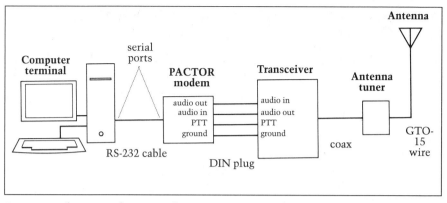

Diagram showing the typical connections used to interconnect a computer, HF transceiver, modem, and antenna for wireless e-mail.

ground and push-to-talk (PTT) connections are the same on both devices.

Using the Winlink 2000 System

When the AirMail 3.0 software is installed, a current listing of all available WL2K stations is loaded into the computer along with their frequencies and locations. Assuming you've installed all the equipment and software correctly, the next step is to get on the air and make contact with any one of the Winlink stations to register with the Winlink system. You will be assigned an Internet address, which will be your amateur radio call sign with "@Winlink.org" added. Once registered with an Internet address, you may start sending e-mail immediately. However, it may take an hour or so before you can receive e-mail as your new Internet address must be propagated throughout the global Winlink network. After you have logged into the system, your call sign will be checked against an amateur call database to ensure your call is valid and that your privileges are appropriate for the amateur radio band used. If this information is not found, you will be asked to provide documentary evidence.

Another great feature of the Winlink system is that once you are registered with the system, you can send and retrieve messages sent to your radio Internet address from any computer with an Internet connection. This can very useful if you're onshore and you want to retrieve your messages at a public library or Internet café.

Weather Information, Amateur Radio, and the Cruising Yachtsman

Weather information is important for the recreational boater, and it's an absolute necessity for the cruising yachtsman. Having a variety of weather information sources available while on an extended cruise can greatly enhance the comfort and safety of the voyage.

E-mail

The HF e-mail system (discussed above) can be used to download weather forecasts from sources such as the Offshore Forecast, the High Seas Forecast, Tropical Cyclone and Coastal broadcasts, Weather Fax Chart Forecasts, and Gridded Binary Data Files (GRIB) Weather Forecasts. Although you cannot directly surf the Internet using the HF e-mail system, you can receive this information by requesting it from a Winlink PMBO. Winlink uses an on-demand bulletin distribution system. Users select the bulletin they want from an available catalog, which currently has more than 700 available weather, propagation, and information bulletins. When a request is received by a PMBO, a copy of the requested information is sent and usually received by the next time the user logs in to the Winlink system. All of the Winlink PMBOs support a single global catalog of bulletins, which ensures that users can access any bulletin from any PMBO worldwide. However, the GRIB forecasts are rather large files and may take 30 minutes or more to download, even with a PACTOR-3 modem.

Voice

Weather voice forecast reports are broadcast over HF, MF, and VHF radio at various times of the day. Voice forecast reports include the Offshore and High Seas reports that are broadcast on HF radio. Offshore forecasts and storm warnings are broadcast by the U.S. Coast Guard on the MF bands. Coastal weather is broadcast by NOAA Weather Radio on the VHF bands. Almost all amateur radio HF radios will receive broadcasts throughout the entire MF and HF bands. They are only limited in the ability to transmit outside the amateur authorized bands.

The Offshore Weather reports are broadcast every 6 hours. The forecast includes a synopsis for the near term and a 5-day extended outlook. The synopsis and outlook have a brief description of significant weather features and forecast over the offshore waters through the forecast period. Emphasis is placed on the forecast movement of low pressure, high pressure, fronts, and tropical storms. The broadcast times (UTC) and frequencies are:

0330 and 0930 on 4,426 kHz, 6,501 kHz, and 8,764 kHz
1600 and 2200 on 6,501 kHz, 8,764 kHz, and 13,089 kHz

Many of the amateur radio marine nets also carry weather reports for various cruising areas. When checking into a marine net, ask if current weather information is available for the area in which you are cruising. Chances are very good that someone on the net can provide you with that information.

Publications on Amateur Radio

American Radio Relay League (ARRL)

The American Radio Relay League is the only nonprofit organization serving the 450,000 amateur radio operators in the United States. The ARRL produces reference manuals, CD-ROMs, and specialty publications as well as its monthly journal, *QST*. Just about any technical or operational information you need to know can be found in an ARRL publication or obtained from its headquarters staff.

The first license manual you should consider is *Now You're Talking!*, 5th ed. This manual provides all the information needed for your first amateur license. *Your Introduction to Morse Code* includes cassette tapes or audio CDs that teach you all of the characters and also give you plenty of practice for the General and Extra Class license exams.

QST *Magazine*

Published monthly since 1914, *QST* is an excellent source of technical, operating, regulatory, and general amateur radio information. *QST* is one of the most significant benefits of ARRL membership.

On-the-Air Bulletins

Up-to-the-minute information of interest to amateurs—such as FCC policy decisions and propagation predictions—is transmitted in W1AW bulletins. W1AW is an amateur radio station maintained at ARRL headquarters in Newington, Connecticut. The station transmits bulletins at regularly scheduled intervals via CW (Morse code), phone (voice), and RTTY (teletype) on various frequencies. A comprehensive Morse-code practice agenda is also transmitted. A detailed schedule of W1AW transmissions appears regularly in *QST* and may also be obtained on request from ARRL. When requesting a schedule, please include a self-addressed, stamped envelope. (Source: *The ARRL Operating Manual*, 8th ed.)

ARRL Publications

ARRL publishes an extensive library of manuals and technical books related to ham radio. Below are just a few publications available from ARRL.

> *Now You're Talking*, 5th ed. (technician license manual)
> *Your Introduction to Morse Code* (2 audio cassettes or CDs)
> *FCC Rule Book*, 13th ed.
> *General Class License Manual*, 5th ed.
> *Extra Class License Manual*, 8th ed.
> *RF Exposure and You*
> *ARRL Operating Manual*, 8th ed.
> *ARRL Repeater Directory*, 2004–2005 ed.
> *ARRL Net Directory*, 2001–2002 ed.
> *ARRL Handbook*, 2005 ed.

Contact Information

For information on ARRL's publications, services, and membership rates, contact:

> American Radio Relay League
> 225 Main Street
> Newington, CT 06111-1494
> (888) 277-5289
> www.arrl.org

Gordon West Publications

These publications include ham test preparation tapes, books, software, and videos.

> THE THEORY on audio cassettes:
> *No-Code Technician* (4 tapes)
> *General Class* (4 tapes)
> *Amateur Extra Class* (4 tapes)

APPENDIX A

THE CODE on audio cassettes:
Learning CW (0–7 wpm, 6 tapes)
Speed Builder (5–16 wpm, 6 tapes)
Speed Builder (10–28 wpm, 6 tapes)

NEW STUDY MANUALS by "Gordo"
No-Code Technician (Element 2)
General Class (Element 3)
Extra Class (Element 4)

PC SOFTWARE with study manuals
No-Code Technician (Element 2)
Tech./Tech.+/General (+Code, Windows)
General Class (3 + Code, Windows)
Extra Class (4 + Code, Windows)
Ham Operator (Tech-Extra + Code)
Morse Software Only

VIDEO VHS with study manual
No-Code Technician Video Course

These materials are available from:

The W5YI Group, Inc.
P.O. Box 565101
Dallas, TX 75356
(800) 669-9594

HamTestOnline

HamTestOnline offers an online study tool that mimics the written exams for all three classes of the amateur radio license. The site tracks your performance and helps you target any weak areas. For more information, go to www.hamtestonline.com.

International Morse Code

At the present time, to take the Amateur Radio Examination for Element 1, you must be able to transmit and receive International Morse Code at 5 wpm. The following characters are required:

- 26 letters of the alphabet
- numerals 0 through 9
- punctuation characters for period, comma, question mark, and fraction bar (slash)
- code symbols for break (BK), end of message (AR), and end of transmission (SK)

For many people, the greatest deterrent to qualifying for an amateur license has been the Morse code requirement. The Technician Class license does not require that you know Morse Code. However, to earn the MF and HF frequency privileges for the General and Amateur Extra Classes, you must pass Element 1 of the code examination by demonstrating Morse code capability. (The required speed is only 5 wpm.)

Learning the code is much easier than most people imagine. Although it does require a serious commitment to the program, many have said that the code can be learned with 24 to 30 hours of effort, spent over a couple of weeks.

There are better ways to learn Morse code than memorizing the alphabet in written form. Numerous audio cassette tapes or compact discs (CDs) use the actual code sounds of the alphanumeric characters and organize them into a message. In fact, some radio operators recommend that you not look at the characters in the written form, but rather learn them by the sound of the character as taught on the various code teaching tapes or CDs that are available.

Some learning schemes break the alphabet, numerals, and punctuation into six groups and work on one group at a time until each group is mastered. For example:

GROUP 1. E T A R L .
GROUP 2. I U F S V ?
GROUP 3. M G Z Q O ,
GROUP 4. K C B D W /
GROUP 5. N Y X P J H
GROUP 6. 1 2 3 4 5 6 7 8 9 0 AR BK SK

Once you have learned the complete list of characters, you can develop code speed in several ways. Cassettes or CDs for advanced speeds are available. Listening to the code practice sessions broadcast by W1AW (the ARRL station) on frequencies in the ham bands can also be helpful. (To get a schedule of their code practice sessions, contact ARRL directly or look in a current issue of QST.)

If you have a PC (or other compatible computer), consider the Morse code program listed in Publications on Amateur Radio (Appendix A). You can select the speed, tone, and type of program. The programs available include beginner character groups and random letters in five-character groups; random letters and numbers, with or without punctuation, in random character groups; and a typical one-sided ham conversation similar to the FCC code test.

Some computer programs even interface with text from data files that you might want to copy for practice. Computer programs set code speeds from 1 or 2 wpm up to 50 wpm. Also, they can slow down the overall speed of characters and words to a wpm rate that is easy for you to copy. This makes it easier for you to increase your speed after you have learned the code.

The following is the complete list of Morse code characters with a phonetic spelling of their sound.

Alphabet

A .-	(dit dah)	N -.	(dah dit)
B -...	(dah dit dit dit)	O ---	(dah dah dah)
C -.-.	(dah dit dah dit)	P .--.	(dit dah dah dit)
D -..	(dah dit dit)	Q --.-	(dah dah dit dah)
E .	(dit)	R .-.	(dit dah dit)
F ..-.	(dit dit dah dit)	S ...	(dit dit dit)
G --.	(dah dah dit)	T -	(dah)
H	(dit dit dit dit)	U ..-	(dit dit dah)
I ..	(dit dit)	V ...-	(dit dit dit dah)
J .---	(dit dah dah dah)	W .--	(dit dah dah)
K -.-	(dah dit dah)	X -..-	(dah dit dit dah)
L .-..	(dit dah dit dit)	Y -.--	(dah dit dah dah)
M --	(dah dah)	Z --..	(dah dah dit dit)

Numerals

0 -----	(dah dah dah dah dah)	5	(dit dit dit dit dit)
1 .----	(dit dah dah dah dah)	6 -....	(dah dit dit dit dit)
2 ..---	(dit dit dah dah dah)	7 --...	(dah dah dit dit dit)
3 ...--	(dit dit dit dah dah)	8 ---..	(dah dah dah dit dit)
4 ....-	(dit dit dit dit dah)	9 ----.	(dah dah dah dah dit)

Punctuation

PERIOD .-.-.- (dit dah dit dah dit dah)
COMMA --..-- (dah dah dit dit dah dah)
QUESTION MARK ..--.. (dit dit dah dah dit dit)
FRACTION BAR (SLASH) -..-. (dah dit dit dah dit)

Code Symbols

BREAK (<u>BK</u>) -...-.- (dah dit dit dit dah dit dah)
END OF MESSAGE (<u>AR</u>) .-.-. (dit dah dit dah dit)
END OF TRANSMISSION (<u>SK</u>) ...-.- (dit dit dit dah dit dah)

The underscores indicate that the letters are sent as one character for these procedural symbols.

Phonetic Alphabet

The International Telecommunication Union recommends the following phonetic alphabet:

A	Alfa (AL fah)	N	November (no VEM ber)
B	Bravo (BRAH voh)	O	Oscar (OSS car)
C	Charlie (CHAR lee)	P	Papa (pah PAH)
D	Delta (DELL tah)	Q	Quebec (keh BECK)
E	Echo (ECK oh)	R	Romeo (ROW me oh)
F	Foxtrot (FOKS trot)	S	Sierra (see AIR rah)
G	Golf (GOLF)	T	Tango (TANG go)
H	Hotel (hoh TELL)	U	Uniform (YOU nee form)
I	India (IN dee ah)	V	Victor (VIK tah)
J	Juliet (JEW lee ETT)	W	Whiskey (WISS key)
K	Kilo (KEY loh)	X	X-Ray (ECKS ray)
L	Lima (LEE mah)	Y	Yankee (YANG key)
M	Mike (MIKE)	Z	Zulu (ZOO loo)

The uppercase letters represent emphasized syllables. Pronunciations shown in this table were designed for speakers from all international languages; consequently, the pronunciations given for "Oscar" and "Victor" may be awkward to English-speaking people in the United States.

R-S-T Reporting System

The R-S-T Reporting System is a means of rating the quality of a signal on a numerical basis; the letters are explained below. The higher the number, the better the signal.

R—readability; rated on a scale of 1 to 5
S—signal strength; rated on a scale of 1 to 9
T—quality of a CW tone; rated on a scale of 1 to 9

Readability

1. Unreadable
2. Barely readable; occasional words distinguishable
3. Readable with considerable difficulty
4. Readable with practically no difficulty
5. Perfectly readable

Signal Strength

1. Faint; signals barely perceptible
2. Very weak signals
3. Weak signals
4. Fair signals
5. Fairly good signals
6. Good signals
7. Moderately strong signals
8. Strong signals
9. Extremely strong signals

Tone

1. Extremely rough; hissing tone
2. Very rough AC note; no trace of musicality
3. Rough, low pitched AC note; slightly musical
4. Rather rough AC note; moderately musical
5. Musically modulated
6. Modulated note; slight trace of whistle
7. Near DC note; smooth ripple
8. Good DC note; just trace of ripple
9. Purest DC note

(If note appears to be crystal controlled, add the letter X after the number indicating tone.)

Q Signals

Listed below are some commonly used "Q signals," whose meanings often need to be expressed with brevity and clarity in amateur communications. When used with Morse code (CW) a Q signal takes the form of a question when it is transmitted followed by the question mark character. When a Q signal is used in voice mode, a question is implied by the interrogative tone of voice. However, without a question mark or interrogative tone, the Q signal serves as a statement. The following table defines the Q signals first as questions, then as statements.

QRG   Will you tell me my exact frequency?/Your exact frequency is _____.

QRK   What is the intelligibility of my signals?/The intelligibility of your signals is __ [1. Bad; 2. Poor; 3. Fair; 4. Good; 5. Excellent].

QRL   Are you busy?/I am busy. Please don't interfere.

QRM   Is my transmission being interfered with?/Your transmission is being interfered with.

QRN   Are you troubled by static?/I am troubled by static.

QRO   Shall I increase power?/Increase power.

QRP   Shall I decrease power?/Decrease power.

QRQ   Shall I send faster?/Send faster.

QRS   Shall I send more slowly?/Send more slowly.

QRT   Shall I stop sending?/Stop sending.

QRU   Have you anything for me?/I have nothing for you.

QRV   Are you ready?/I am ready.

QRZ   Who is calling me?/You are being called by _____.

QSA   What is the strength of my signals?/The strength of your signals is __ [1. Scarcely perceptible; 2. Weak; 3. Fairly good; 4. Good; 5. Very good].

QSB   Are my signals fading?/Your signals are fading.

QSK   Can I break in during your transmission?/Break in on my transmission.

QSL   Can you acknowledge receipt?/I am acknowledging receipt.

QSO   Can you communicate with ____ direct?/I can communicate with ____ direct.

QSP   Will you relay to ____ ?/I will relay to ____.

QSY   Shall I change to transmission on another frequency?/Change to transmission on another frequency.

QTH   What is your location?/My location is _____.

QTR   What is the correct time?/The time is _____.

Operating in Other Countries

Reciprocal Operating Agreements

The United States has negotiated reciprocal operating agreements with many countries. After obtaining a permit from the host country, amateurs may operate within one of these countries according to the terms of the agreement. The sole exception is Canada, where amateurs with valid U.S. or Canadian licenses may operate within the other country's territory without obtaining a permit. They must abide by all the terms of the agreement.

These countries have reciprocal operating agreements with the United States:

Antigua and Barbuda	Denmark (including Greenland) (1)	India
Argentina (2)	Dominican Republic	Indonesia
Australia	Dominica	Ireland (1)
Austria (1)	Ecuador	Israel
Bahamas	El Salvador	Italy (1)
Barbados	Federated States of Micronesia	Jamaica
Belgium (1)		Japan
Belize	Fiji	Jordan
Bolivia	Finland (1)	Kiribati
Bosnia-Herzegovina (1)	France and Territories* (1)	Kuwait
Botswana	Germany (1)	Liberia
Brazil (2)	Greece	Luxembourg (1)
Canada (2)	Grenada	Macedonia
Chile	Guatemala	Marshall Islands**
Colombia	Guyana	Mexico
Costa Rica	Haiti	Monaco (1)
Croatia	Honduras	Netherlands (1)
Cyprus (1)	Iceland (1)	Netherlands Antilles (1)
		New Zealand

Nicaragua	St. Vincent	Thailand
Norway (1)	Seychelles	Trinidad & Tobago
Panama	Sierra Leone	Turkey (1)
Papua-New Guinea	Solomon Islands	Tuvalu
Paraguay	South Africa	United Kingdom**
Peru (2)	Spain (1)	(1)
Philippines	Suriname	Uruguay (2)
Portugal (1)	Sweden (1)	Venezuela (2)
St. Lucia	Switzerland (1)	

Notes: Since there is an automatic reciprocal agreement between the United States and Canada, there is no need to apply for a permit. Simply sign your U.S. call followed by a slant bar and the Canadian letter/number identifier.

(1) Indicates countries that are included in the CERT countries list. These countries accept HF and VHF operation and are available to Technician Plus, General, Advanced, and Extra Class amateurs. The U.S. Novice Class is not eligible for CERT operation.

(2) Indicates Interamerican Telecommunications Commission (CITEL) countries. These are Central and South American countries that allow U.S. amateurs to operate provided they obtain an International Amateur Radio Permit.

European Conference of Postal and Telecommunications Administrations (CEPT)

In addition to the reciprocal operating agreements, the United States has obtained permission for U.S. FCC-licensed amateurs to operate in CEPT countries. The CEPT radio amateur permit is

---

*Includes French Guiana, French Polynesia, Guadeloupe, Saint-Paul Island, Crozet Island, Kerguelen Island, Martinique, St. Pierre and Miquelon, and Wallis and Futuna Islands.

**Includes Bermuda, British Virgin Islands, Cayman Islands, Channel Islands (including Guernsey and Jersey), Falkland Islands (including South Sandwich Island), Gibraltar, Isle of Man, Montserrat, St. Helena including Ascension Island, Gough Island, Tristan da Cunha Island, Northern Ireland, and the Turks and Caicos Islands.

available if the U.S. ham carries an original U.S. license, a U.S. passport, and a copy of the FCC 92s Public Notice. This notice is printed in three languages: English, French, and German. Those countries on the reciprocal operating agreement list, marked (1), are included in the CEPT countries list. These countries accept HF and VHF operation and are available to amateurs with Technician Plus, General, Advanced, and Extra Class licenses. They accept VHF only for Technician Class hams. The U.S. Novice Class amateur is not eligible for CEPT operation.

The following countries are in addition to the reciprocal operating agreement list:

Azores (1)	Guiana (1)	Reunion (1)
Bulgaria (1)	Hungary (1)	Romania (1)
Czech Republic (1)	Latvia (1)	St. Bartholomew (1)
Corsica (1)	Liechtenstein (1)	St. Martin (1)
Estonia (1)	Lithuania (1)	Slovak Republic (1)
Faroe Islands (1)	Madeira (1)	Slovenia (1)
French Antarctica (1)	Mayotte (1)	

APPENDIX F

International Amateur Radio Permit (IARP)

An International Amateur Radio Permit (IARP) is available for U.S. amateur operations from some Central and South American areas. The permit allows U.S. amateurs to operate in an Interamerica Telecommunications Commission (CITEL) country. Participating IARP countries are: Argentina, Brazil, Canada, Peru, United States, Uruguay, and Venezuela. These countries are identified with "(2)" in the reciprocal operating agreements list. As with CEPT, the IARP allows operation on the HF and VHF bands for any U.S. amateur holding a valid Technician Plus, General, Advanced, or Amateur Extra Class license. It allows operation above 30 MHz (VHF) for those amateurs holding a Technician Class license. Novice Class amateurs are not eligible. Permits under this service describe the authority in four different languages and are available from the ARRL, a member-society of the International Amateur Radio Union (IARU).

International Third-Party Traffic

The FCC defines third-party traffic as "amateur radio communication by or under the supervision of the control operator at an amateur radio station to another amateur radio station on behalf of anyone other than the control operators." U.S. amateurs are permitted to handle such traffic only with countries having third-party agreements with the United States. Here is a current list of these countries:

Antigua and Barbuda	Gambia, The	Paraguay
Argentina	Ghana	Peru
Australia	Grenada	Philippines
Belize	Guatemala	Pitcairn Island*
Boliva	Guyana	St. Christopher/
Bosnia-Herzegovina	Haiti	Nevis
Brazil	Honduras	St. Lucia
Canada	Israel	St. Vincent/
Chile	ITU, Geneva	Grenadines
Colombia	VIC, Vienna	Sierra Leone
Comoros (Federal Is-	Jamaica	South Africa
lamic Republic of)	Jordan	Swaziland
Costa Rica	Liberia	Trinidad/Tobago
Cuba	Marshall Islands	Turkey
Dominican Republic	Mexico	United Kingdom**
Dominica	Micronesia	Uruguay
Ecuador	Nicaragua	Venezuela
El Salvador	Panama	

*Since 1970, there has been an informal agreement between the United Kingdom and the United States permitting Pitcairn and U.S. amateurs to exchange messages concerning medical emergencies, urgent need for equipment or supplies, and private or personal matters of island residents.

**Limited to special-event stations, with call sign prefix GB. (GB3 excluded.)

U.S. amateurs may operate in the following territories under their FCC license:

Northern Marianas Islands	Kure Island	Commonwealth of Puerto Rico
Guam	American Samoa	U.S. Virgin Islands
Johnson Island	Wake Island	
Midway Island	Wilkes Island	
	Peale Island	

At the end of an exchange of third-party traffic with a station located in a foreign country, an FCC-licensed amateur must transmit the call sign of the foreign station as well as his/her own call sign.

APPENDIX G

Volunteer Examiner Coordinators

Persons who wish to take an examination for Technician, General, or Extra Class amateur operator licenses should contact amateur operators in their area who are accredited as volunteer examiners (VEs) by any of the following national volunteer examiner coordinators (VECs):

Anchorage Amateur Radio Club
HC01 Box 6139-C
Palmer, AK 99645-9604
(907) 746-3996

American Radio Relay League
225 Main Street
Newington, CT 06111
(860) 594-0200

Central America CAVEC
1215 Dale Drive SE
Huntsville, AL 35801-2031
(205) 536-3904

Golden Empire ARS
P.O. Box 508
Chico, CA 95927-0508
(530) 345-3515

Greater Los Angeles ARG
9737 Noble Avenue
North Hills, CA 91343-2403
(818) 892-2068

Jefferson Amateur Radio Club
P.O. Box 24368
New Orleans, LA 70184-4368

Laurel Amateur Radio Club, Inc.
P.O. Box 3039
Laurel, MD 20709-3039
(301) 317-7819

WECA
Westchester Emergency Communications Association, Inc.
P.O. Box 831
Sleepy Hollow, NY 10591-0831
(914) 741-6606

Milwaukee Radio Amateurs Club
7835 W. Caldwell Court
Milwaukee, WI 53218-3526
(414) 466-4267

MO-KAN VEC
P.O. Box 11
Liberty, MO 64068-0011
(816) 781-7313

SANDARC
P.O. Box 2446
La Mesa, CA 91943-2446
(619) 697-1475

Sunnyvale VEC Amateur Radio
   Club
P.O. Box 60307
Sunnyvale, CA 94088-0307
(408) 255-9000

Western Carolina WCARS
6702 Matterhorn Court
Knoxville, TN 37918-6314
(423) 687-5410

W4VEC, Inc.
3504 Stonehurst Place
High Point, NC 27265-2106
(336) 841-7576

W5YI-VEC
P.O. Box 565101
Dallas, TX 75356-5101
(800) 669-9594

APPENDIX

H

APPENDIX ❶

Maritime Mobile Nets

The Intercontinental Traffic Net and the Maritime Mobile Service Net both meet on 14,300 kHz so there is just about a 24-hour-a-day watch. Many nets listed are not primarily M/M nets but may run maritime mobile traffic. Some follow daylight savings time change.

WORLDWIDE HAM NETS AVAILABLE FOR THE MARITIME MOBILE AMATEUR

TIME (UTC/GMT)	FREQUENCY (kHz)	NET NAME	DAYS
0100	3,935	Gulf Coast Hurricane Net	Daily
0100	21,407	PAC-IND Ocean Net	Daily
0100	14,300	Maritime Mobile Service Net	Daily
0200	3,992	Arizona Traffic Net	Daily
0200	14,305	Cal-Hawaii Net	Daily
0200	7,290	Hawaii PM Net	M–F
0220	14,315	John's Weather Net	Daily
0300	14,313	Seafarer's Net	Daily
0300	14,106	Traveler's Net	Daily
0330	14,040	E/C M/M CW Net	Daily
0400	14,115	Canadian DDD Net	Daily
0400	14,075	PAC CW Traffic Net	M-W-F
0400	14,314	Pacific Maritime Mobile Net	Daily
0500	21,200	VK/NZ African Net	Daily
0500	14,280	USA/Australia Traffic Net	Daily
0530	14,303	Swedish Maritime Net	Daily
0530	14,314	Pacific Maritime Net	Daily
0630	14,180	Pitcairn Net	F
0630	14,320	South African Maritime Net	Daily

102

TIME (UTC/GMT)	FREQUENCY (kHz)	NET NAME	DAYS
0700	14,300	International M/M Net	Daily
0700	14,265	Pacific Island Net	Daily
0700	14,310	Guam Area Net	Daily
0715	3,820	Bay Of Islands Net	Daily
0800	7,280	Australia Traffic Net	Daily
0800	14,315	Pacific Inter-Island Net	Daily
0800	14,303	UK Maritime Net	Daily
0900	14,300	Mediterranean M/M Net	Daily
0900	7,080	Canary Island Net	Daily
1000	14,330	Pacific Gunkholers Net	Daily
1000	14,300	German Maritime Mobile Net	Daily
1030	3,815	Caribbean Weather Net	Daily
1030	14,265	Barbados Cruising Net	Daily
1100	3,750	Maritime Weather Net	Daily
1100	7,230	Caribbean M/M Net	Daily
1100	14,300	Intercontinental Traffic Net	Daily
1100	14,283	Friendly Caribus Connection	Daily
1130	14,320	South African M/M Net	Daily
1130	21,325	South Atlantic Roundtable	Daily
1200	14,040	Maritime Mobile CW Net	Daily
1200	14,332	Young Ladies Emergency Net	Daily
1200	14,320	Southeast Asia net	Daily
1245	7,268	East Coast Waterway Net	Daily
1300	21,400	Transatlantic M/M Net	Daily
1400	7,292	Florida Coast Net	Daily
1400	3,963	Sonrisa Net	Daily
1500	7,193	Alaska Net	Daily
1545	14,340	Marquesas Net	Daily
1600	7,238.5	Baja California Maritime Net	Daily
1600	14,313	Coast Guard M/M Net	M–F
1630	7,285	Serape Net	Sun
1630	21,350	Pitcairn Net	F
1630	14,340	California/Hawaiian Net	M–F

APPENDIX

TIME (UTC/GMT)	FREQUENCY (kHz)	NET NAME	DAYS
1700	7,240	Bajco M/M Net	M–F
1700	14,300	International M/M Net	Daily
1700	14,287	USPS-CPS Net	Sat
1700	14,329	Skippers Net	Daily
1730	14,292	Alaska Net	M–F
1730	14,115	Canadian DDD Net	M–F
1800	14,285	Kaffee Klatch UN-NE	M-W-Sat
1800	14,300	Maritime Mobile Service Net	Daily
1800	14,303	UK Maritime Net	Daily
1800	7,076	South Pacific Cruising Net	Daily
1800	7,197	South Pacific Sailing Net	Daily
1830	14,342	Manana M/M Net Warm Up	M–Sat
1900	14,305	Confusion Net	M–F
1900	14,342	Manana M/M Net	M–Sat
1900	7,255	West Pacific Net	Daily
1900	7,285	Shamaru Net	Daily
1900	21,390	Halo Net	Daily
1900	14,329	Bay Of Islands Net	Daily
1900	3,855	Friendly Net	Daily
1900	3,990	Northwest Maritime Net	Daily
2000	7,060	VK Maritime Net	Daily
2030	14,303	Swedish Maritime Net	Daily
2100	14,315	Tony's Net	Daily
2100	21,390	North-South Americas Net	Daily
2130	14,318	Daytime Pacific Net	Daily
2130	14,290	East Coast Waterway Net	Daily
2200	21,350	Pitcairn Net	Tues
2200	21,404	Pacific Maritime Net Warmup	M–F
2230	3,815	Caribbean Weather Net	Daily
2230	21,404	15 Mtr Pacific Maritime Net	M–F
2300	14,300	Intercontinental Traffic Net	Daily
2310	14,285	Cal-South Pacific Net	M
2330	21,325	South Atlantic Roundtable	Daily
2400	14,320	SEA Maritime Mobile Net	Daily

Partial List of Coastal 2-Meter Repeaters

Alabama	Mobile	146.895–
California	Crescent City	146.880–
	Eureka	147.000–
	Long Beach	146.790–
	Monterey	145.430–
	Newport Beach	145.420–
	San Clemente	146.025+
	San Diego	145.160+
	San Francisco	145.150– autopatch
	San Luis Obispo	146.800–
	Santa Barbara	147.945– autopatch
	Santa Cruz	145.250–
Connecticut	Bridgeport	146.895– autopatch
	New London	146.970– autopatch
Florida	Boca Raton	146,820–
	Clearwater	145.110–
	Cocoa Beach	145.370–
	Englewood	146.700–
	Fort Myers	146.760– autopatch
	Ft. Lauderdale (S)	146.850–
	Ft. Lauderdale (N)	146.610–
	Jacksonville	146.760– autopatch
	Key Largo	147.165+ autopatch
	Key West	146.940–
	Marathon	147.255+
	Melbourne	145.470– autopatch
	Miami/Biscayne Bay	146.775– autopatch
	Panama City	146.940– autopatch
	Pensacola	145.350– autopatch
	Punta Gorda	146.745– autopatch
	Riviera Beach	147.075+ autopatch

	St. Petersburg	147.120+ autopatch
	Stuart	147.060+
Georgia	Brunswick	146.730– autopatch
	Savannah	146.970– autopatch
Louisiana	New Orleans	147.240+ autopatch
Maine	Bar Harbor	145.290–
	Portland	146.730+
Maryland	Annapolis	147.105+ autopatch
Massachusetts	Gloucester	145.130–
	Nantucket	145.310–
	Provincetown	147.255+
Mississippi	Gulfport	147.375+
New Hampshire	Portsmouth	145.150–
New Jersey	Atlantic City	146.985–
	Brigantine	146.985–
	Cape May	147.285+
New York	Manhattan	145.270–
North Carolina	Albemarle	146.985– autopatch
	Beaufort	145.310–
	Wilmington	146.730– autopatch
Oregon	Astoria	146.660– autopatch
	Myrtle Point	145.190–
	Newport	147.300+ autopatch
South Carolina	Charleston	147.250– autopatch
	Myrtle Beach	147.120+ autopatch
Texas	Corpus Christi	146.880– autopatch
	Galveston	146.680–
	Seabrook	147.260+
	South Padre Island	147.240+
Virginia	Norfolk	145.330–
Washington	Friday Harbor	146.900– autopatch
	Puget Sound (N)	145.250–
	Puget Sound (S)	147.240+
Bahamas	Nassau	146.940–
	Treasure Cay	145.210–

The above are repeater transmitting frequencies. The +/– signs are for the 600 kHz offset for the repeater access. For example, the Annapolis repeater transmits on 147.105 MHz. Adjust the 2-meter handheld to that frequency and listen for an identification signal

APPENDIX

from the repeater. Adjust the offset switch on the handheld to the + position. This means that when the handheld's transmit switch is depressed, it will transmit on 147.705 MHz. If the handheld transceiver is within range of the repeater antenna, the repeater should transmit an acknowledging signal upon release of the handheld transmit switch. The standard offset frequency for all 2-meter repeaters is 600 kHz (0.6 MHz).

Because of the increasing popularity of paging systems, it has become necessary for many repeaters to implement a system of tone access. This is a sub-audible tone that is transmitted by the user and will hold the repeater on the air as long as the tone is present. See the Repeater Directory for identification of the tone frequencies used.

Repeaters are owned by individual amateurs, amateur radio clubs, and repeater clubs. All repeaters must be under an amateur radio control operator. Computers run repeaters that have been installed at remote locations.

Once you've accessed a repeater, make a statement such as "This is WR4XXX listening." Most repeaters have local hams who leave their rigs tuned to the repeater. When they hear such a call, they frequently respond.

There is no assurance that the above repeater list is functional all the time. Repeaters at remote locations are subject to lightning strikes, vandalism, and mechanical breakdowns.

Repeaters are used in numerous other bands in addition to 2 meters. These bands include 10 meters, 6 meters, 1.25 meters, 70 centimeters, 33 centimeters, 23 centimeters and above.

A listing of repeaters (across all bands, including repeaters for amateur television) in North, Central, and South America is included in *The ARRL Repeater Directory*, 2003–2004 edition. Roughly 21,000 repeater stations are listed in this publication.

APPENDIX

Partial List of Participating Mail Box Offices (PMBOs)

Austria	OE4XBU	Eisenstadt
Australia	VK8HF	Darwin
	VK6KPS	Perth
Canada	VE6KBS	Calgary, Alberta
	VE2AFQ	Montreal
Caribbean	WG3G	Trinidad
	ZF1GC	Grand Cayman Island
	NP2E	St. Thomas, Virgin Islands
Germany	DA5UAW	Rudolstadt
Italy	IV3XHR	Udine
Middle East	A71BY	Qatar
Netherlands	PA3DUV	Netherlands
New Zealand	ZL1MA	Auckland
	ZL2UT	Gisborne
South Africa	ZS5S	Howick
Sweden	SM6USU	Glose
Thailand	HS0AC	Bangkok

United States	AB7AA	Oahu, Hawaii
	AH6QK	Oahu, Hawaii
	K6CYC	Los Angeles, California
	W6IM	San Diego, California
	K6IXA	Atwater, California
	K4CJX	Nashville, Tennessee
	K4SET	Murray, Kentucky
	KA7CTT	Vancouver, Washington
	KB6YNO	South Portland, Maine
	KN6KB	Rockledge, Florida
	N8PGR	North Royalton, Ohio
	N0IA	Deltona, Florida
	W1ON	Bedford, Massachusetts
	W7BO	Woodland, Washington
	W9MR	Keensburg, Illinois
	W9GSS	East Peoria, Illinois
	WA2DXQ	Ft. Lauderdale, Florida
	WB0TAX	Elm Grove, Louisiana
	WB5KSD	Farmersville, Texas
	WD8DHF	Harker Heights, Texas

APPENDIX

Authorized SCS PACTOR Modem Dealers

PTC -II USB + PACTOR-3 ~ $1100

California

Baytronics South
11315 Washington Place
Los Angeles, CA 90066
www.baytronics.com
Phone: (310) 915-1616
Fax: (310) 915-1973

Farallon Electronics
(Also North American
distributor)
2346 Mainship Way, Suite 101
Sausalito, CA 94965
www.yachtwire.com
Phone: (415) 331-1924
Fax: (415) 331-2063

H.F. Radio On Board
1813 Clement Avenue #24
Alameda, CA 94501
www.hfradio.com
Phone: (510) 814-8888
Fax: (510) 769-1573

Hi-Tek PC Solutions
42880 Joshua Tree Court
Murieta, CA 92562
www.hitekpc.com
Phone: (909) 461-8528

Johnson Hicks Marine
333 Lake Avenue #C
Santa Cruz, CA 95062
E-mail: jhme6@cs.com
Phone: (831) 475-3383
Fax: (831) 475-1498

Long Beach Marine Electronics
6400 Marina Drive #4
Long Beach, CA 90803
www.longbeachmarine.com
Phone: (562) 594-8888
Fax: (562) 799-1102

Maritime Communications Inc.
766 Washington Boulevard
Marina Del Rey, CA 90292
E-mail: marcomm@aol.com
Phone: (310) 821-4958
Fax: (310) 821-9591

Maritime Electronics of Sausalito
300 Harbor Drive
Sausalito, CA 94965
www.maritimeelectronics.com
Phone: (415) 332-5086
Fax: (415) 332-6344

Offshore Outfitters
1273 Scott Street, Suite D
San Diego, CA 92016

www.offshoreoutfitters.com
Phone: (619) 225-5690
Fax: (619) 509-2082

Voyager Marine Radio
829 Harbor Island Drive
Newport Beach, CA 92660
E-mail: captwade@adelphia.net
Phone: (760) 365-0901
Fax: (760) 285-9929

Connecticut

Custom Navigation
633 Boston Post Road
Westbrook, CT 06498
www.customnav.com
Phone: (860) 399-5511
Fax: (860) 399-5683

Florida

Dockside Radio
Punta Gorda, FL
www.docksideradio.com
Phone: (619) 890-4533

MarineNet Wireless
17940 Loxahatchee River Road
Jupiter, FL 33458
www.marinenet.net
Phone: (561) 747-5686
Fax: (561) 747-9357

Mike's Electronics
1001 NW 52 Street
Ft. Lauderdale, FL 33309
E-mail: mspivak@bellsouth.net
Phone: (800) 427-3066
Fax: (954) 491-7011

Miller Marine
4228 Lakeside Drive
Jacksonville, FL 32210
www.millermarine.com
Phone: (904) 388-3690
Fax: (904) 389-8555

Sea Wiz Marine
2250 Overseas Highway
Marathon, FL 33050
www.seawizmarine.com
Phone (305) 289-4044
Fax: (305) 289-3090

SeaTech Systems
1160 Serpentine Drive South
St. Petersburg, FL 33705
www.sea-tech.com
Phone: (727) 865-0159

Hawaii

Navtech Marine Electronics
965 B North Nimitz Highway
Honolulu, HI 96817
www.navtechmarine.com
Phone: (808) 536-3700
Fax: (808) 536-7656

Maine

Marine Computer Systems
58 Fore Street
Portland, ME 04101
www.marinecomputer.com
Phone: (207) 871-1575
Fax: (207) 871-1834

Michigan

Off-Shore Marine
6883 4 Mile Road NE
Ada, MI 49301

APPENDIX F

111

E-mail: scenano@earthlink.net
Phone: (616) 890-1407
Fax: (619) 954-9866

New Hampshire
Navtronics, LLC
131 Mirona Road
Portsmouth, NH 03801
www.navtronics.com
Phone: (603) 436-2544
Fax: (603) 436-2591

New York
RadCom Technologies
509 Center Avenue
Mamaroneck, NY 10543
www.radcommarine@aol.com
Phone: (914) 698-6800
Fax: (914) 698-6801

Oregon
Rodgers Marine Electronics
3445 NE Marine Drive
Portland, OR 97211
E-mail: rodgersmarine.com
Phone: (503) 287-1101
Fax: (503) 288-3745

Pennsylvania
Marine Computer Systems
19 Walnut Lane
Salford, PA 18957
www.marinecomputer.com
Phone: (610) 287-0703
Fax: (847) 589-6550

Rhode Island
Custom Navigation
1 Lagoon Road, Suite 5

Portsmouth, RI 02806
E-mail: sggill@compuserve.com
Phone: (401) 683-6005
Fax: (401) 683-6007

Texas
Sea Tech Systems
P.O. Box 1352
Kemah, TX 77565
www.sea-tech.com
Phone: (800) 444-2581
Fax: (281) 334-3320

Washington, D.C.
Cruising Services and Supplies
2307 Huidekoper Place NW
Washington, D.C. 20007
E-mail: CruisingServices@
  aol.com
Phone: (800) 308-0739
Fax: (202) 342-0191

Washington State
Emerald City Marine
1900 N. Northlake Way, Suite
  113
Seattle, WA 98103
www.emeraldmarine.com
Phone: (206) 547-8171
Fax: (206) 547-3407

The Offshore Store
3400 Stone Way
Seattle, WA 98103
www.offshorestore.net
Phone: (206) 632-3025
Fax: (206) 632-0971

Partial List of Equipment and Parts Suppliers

Amateur Radio Equipment Manufacturers

Alinco
15 South Trade Center
   Parkway, #B5
Conroe, TX 77385
(936) 271-3366
www.alinco.com

Elecraft
P.O. Box 69
Aptos, CA 95001
(831) 662-8345
www.elecraft.com

ICOM
2380 116th Ave NE
Bellevue, WA 98004
(425) 454-8155
www.icomamerica.com

KENWOOD
2201 East Dominguez Street
Long Beach, CA 90801
(310) 639-4200
www.kenwood.net

TEN-TEC
1185 Dolly Parton Parkway
Sevierville, TN 37862

(800) 833-7373
www.tentec.com

YAESU
10900 Walker Street
Cypress, CA 90630
(714) 827-7600
www.vxstdusa.com

Amateur Radio Parts and Equipment Suppliers

Amateur Electronic Supply (AES)
www.aesham.com

   Milwaukee, WI 53223
   (800) 559-0411

   Orlando, FL
   (800) 327-1917

   Cleveland, OH
   (800) 321-3594

   Las Vegas, NV
   (800) 634-6227

Burghardt Amateur Center
710 10th Street SW
Watertown, SD 57201
(605) 886-7314
www.burghardt-amateur.com

Ham Radio Outlet
www.hamradio.com
(Stores located in California,
Delaware, Oregon, Colorado,
Georgia, Virginia, and New
Hampshire. Toll-free tele-
phone numbers are listed by
area.)
West: (800) 854-6046
Mountain: (800) 444-9476
Southeast: (800) 444-7927
Mid-Atlantic: (800) 444-4799
Northeast: (800) 644-4476
New England: (800) 444-0047

Mouser Electronics
1000 N Main Street
Mansfield, TX 6063
(800) 346-6873
www.mouser.com

R&L Electronics
1315 Maple Avenue
Hamilton, OH 45011
(800) 221-7735
www.randl.com

RadioShack
See their catalog for stores in
most major cities.
(800) 442-7221
www.radioshack.com

Antenna Tuners

Ameritron
116 Willow Road
Starkville, MS 39759
(662) 323-8211
www.ameritron.com

LDG Electronics, Inc.
1445 Parran Road
St. Leonard, MD 20685
(410) 586-2177
www.ldgelectronics.com

MFJ Enterprises, Inc.
300 Industrial Park Road
Starkville, MS 39795
(662) 323-5869
www.mfj@mfjenterprises.com

SGC, Inc.
13737 SE 26th Street
Bellevue, WA 98005
(800) 259-7331
www.sgcworld.com

Marine Vertical Antennas

Shakespeare Electronic Products
3801 Westmore Drive
Columbia, SC 29223
(803) 276-5504
www.shakespeare-marine.com

BoatUS
See their catalog for nationwide
store listing.
Main Store: 880 S. Pickett Street
Alexandria, VA 22304-9832
(800) 283-2883
www.BoatUS.com

West Marine
See their catalog for nationwide
listing.
(800) 262-8464
www.westmarine.com

APPENDIX

Rigging Isolators, Copper Mesh/Strap, GTO-15 Antenna Lead-In Wire

Navtec Corporation
351 New Whitfield Street
Guilford, CT 06437
(203) 458-3163
www.navtec.net/home/index.cfm

Sta-Lok Terminals Ltd.
Unit 6, Causeway End, Station
    Road
Lawford, Essex CO11 1AA,
England
+44-0-1206-391509
www.stalok.com
(Check their website for a
    worldwide distributors list.)

Newmar Corporation
2911 W. Garry Avenue
Santa Ana, CA 92704
(714) 751-0488
www.newmarpower.com

West Marine
See their catalog for nationwide
    store list.
(800) 262-8464
www.westmarine.com

Glossary

Airmail: Radio e-mail software designed by Jim Corenman for use with programs like Winlink 2000

amateur radio: A radio communication service authorized by the FCC for two-way private communication between individuals. Amateur radio is a scientific hobby, a means of gaining skill in the art and science of electronics, and an opportunity to communicate worldwide with fellow amateur radio operators by private shortwave radio

amateur radio bands: The frequencies between 1.8 MHz and 29.7 MHz that are allocated to the Amateur Radio Service by the FCC

amateur radio operator: A person holding a license to operate an amateur radio station

Amateur Radio Service: Another name for amateur radio

amateur radio station: A station licensed in the amateur radio service. Also the necessary equipment used for amateur communication

alternating current: An electrical current that reverses direction of flow at regular time intervals

alternator: A device that generates an alternating voltage by rotating a coil through a magnetic field, or by rotating a magnetic field inside a stationary coil

ampere: The unit of measurement of current flow. The symbol for current in amperes in equations is (I)

amplitude modulation (AM): The process of impressing information on a radio frequency signal by varying its amplitude in accordance with the amplitude of the information to be transmitted

anode: The positive electrode toward which negative ions are drawn

antenna: A wire, rod, or other assembly designed to transmit or receive radio signals

backstay: Part of the standing rigging on a sailboat, usually cable, that supports the mast

baud rate: A measure of the speed of serial communication using a modem device

bits per second: A standard measure of data transmission speed

116

bonding: The process of electrically tying together all major fixed metal items on a boat

bonding ground: A conductor that connects all metallic structures, tanks, and other equipment on a boat to maintain a common local (earth) ground. Used to control galvanic corrosion and disperse lightning strikes

coaxial cable: A transmission line in which one conductor completely surrounds the other, the two being coaxial and separated by a dielectric. There is no external radiated field, and the line is not susceptible to other external fields

counterpoise: Sometimes referred to as a ground plane. It is usually composed of copper mesh or strap to provide a radio frequency (RF) ground for an antenna system

coupler: A device used to couple a transmitted radio signal to an antenna system; also referred to as an antenna tuner. Couplers can be either manual or automatic

DIN plug: DIN stands for for Deutsches Institut für Normung, the German Institute for Standardization. A standard connector used to connect devices such as modems and audio equipment

direct current: An electrical current of either constant or variable magnitude that flows in one direction only

earth ground: A point that is at the same electrical potential as the surrounding earth

e-mail: Electronic mail that is transmitted via the Internet

frequency: The number of cycles per second of an electromagnetic wave measured in hertz

frequency range: A portion of the electromagnetic spectrum, for example, the frequencies used for radio and radar

galvanic corrosion: Destruction of metal caused by the current flow that occurs when two different metals are electrically connected and immersed in an electrolyte

ground plane: See counterpoise

ground wave: A radio wave traveling essentially parallel to the earth's surface

ham radio: Amateur radio licensed for noncommercial use. *See also* amateur radio

half-wave dipole: A radio antenna that has two parts (poles) exactly equal in length and which the overall length of the antenna is a one-half wavelength of the operating frequency

hertz: A measure of frequency: 1 hertz is equal to 1 cycle per second

impedance: The total opposition that a circuit offers to the flow of alternating current due to the combined effects of resistance and reactance

modem: A device or program that transmits data. Sometimes used to enable a computer to convert analog information to digital data

Morse code: A system of digital pulses used to communicate. Invented by Samuel Morse

PACTOR: A mode of communication that uses frequency shift keying

peak envelope power: The average power of a radio frequency cycle having the greatest amplitude

PMBO (Participating Mail Box Operators): The system used by the Winlink Program to transmit and receive e-mail via amateur HF radio

propagation: The outward radiation of RF energy from an antenna into space. As the RF energy travels through space, its strength varies inversely as the square of the distance from the antenna

QSL cards: Postcards that serve as a confirmation of communication between two amateur radio operators

radio frequencies: Electromagnetic frequencies that range from 10 kHz to 300 GHz and can travel through space

receiver: A device that converts radio signals into a form that can be heard or seen

repeater: An amateur station that receives a radio signal and retransmits it for greater range. Repeater stations are usually located on towers, tall buildings, or mountain tops

shortwave: A term used to describe a portion of the radio frequency spectrum normally considered from 3 to 30 MHz

single sideband (SSB): A radio transmission mode where the carrier and one sideband of the amplitude modulated (AM) mode has been suppressed

sky wave: Radio waves refracted back to earth from the ionosphere

solar flux index: A gauge of solar particles and magnetic fields radiated from the sun and reaching the earth's atmosphere

transceiver: A radio set that combines transmitting and receiving modes in one package. It may have circuits or components common to both the receiver and transmitter

transmitter: A device that produces radio frequency signals

tropospheric propagation conditions: The conditions of the troposphere that support the refraction and scattering of radio waves above 30 MHz

Winlink 2000: The amateur radio high-frequency wireless e-mail service provider

Index

Numbers in **bold** refer to pages with illustrations

AC generators, 38
ACK, 29
Airmail 3.0 (software), 78, 79–80, 81
Amateur Extra Class License, 10, 19
amateur radio: advantages to boaters, 2–3; equipment component compatibility with marine radio, 3–4; historical development, 4–7; limitations, 1–2
Amateur Radio E-mail Provider, 77
Amateur Radio Emergency Service (ARES), 13
amateur radio frequencies, 58, 65–67
amateur radio objectives: advancement in the art, 11–12; emergency or public service communication, 11; individual skill advancement, 12; international goodwill, 13; reserve pool of skilled operators, 12–13
Amateur Teleprinting Over Radio (AMTOR), 29
American Boat and Yacht Council (ABYC), 34
American Radio Relay League (ARRL), 2, 6–7, 84, 85
amplitude modulation (AM) of telephony, 14
AMTOR. *See* Amateur Teleprinting Over Radio (AMTOR)
antenna: as sailboat's backstay rigging, 43, **44**, 45, **46**, 47; connections, 48–49; height, 43, 45; insulation, **46**; space restrictions, 43–47; systems for HF, 47–48; systems for VHF bands, 39–40, 49; tuners, 47–48; tuners, automatic, 55–56
ARRL Repeater Directory, The (ARRL), 107
attenuator, 55
autopatch capability, 73
awards: DX Century Club, 22; WAC, 22; WAS, 23

backstay antenna insulation, **46**
band lengths, 7
band propagation conditions: 2-meter, 70–71; 6-meter, 70; 10-meter, 70; 12-meter, 70; 15-meter, 70; 17-meter, 70; 20-meter, 69; 30-meter, 69; 40-meter, 69; 60-meter, 69; 80-meter, 68–69; 160-meter, 68
bands, 62
battery power setup, **39**
boaters. *See* cruising
bonding system, 40
Bowdoin (schooner), 11

call signs: issuance of, 19–20; usage during transmissions, 58
Canadian Power and Sail Squadrons Amateur Radio Net: net schedule, 76; 20-meter band, 69
carrier wave (CW) transmissions, 28–29
CB lingo, 58–59
channels, 55
coastal cruising applications of ham radio, 72–73
Coastal 2-meter repeaters, 105–7
coax cable, 48
Commission Registration Systems (CORES), 17
communications modes, 14–15
computers: e-mail access setup and adapters, **80–81**
contact range, 7
contests: distance transmission (DX), 14; Field Day, 24; "Islands on the Air," 12; Sweepstakes, 24–25; types, 24; VHF and Microwave, 25. *See also* awards
control switches, 31–52; antenna installation, 43–47; antennas for VHF bands, 49; antenna systems for bands below VHF, 39–40; antenna tuner, 47–48; cables and connections, 48–49; equipment selection, 32–37; land mobile operation, 49–51; mobile operations, 38–**39**; mode switch, 57; planning, 31; portable operation, 51–52; RF ground system, 40–43; station installation, 34–37
Corenman, Jim, 79
CORES (Commission Registration System), 17
counterpoise, 40, 41, **42**
CQ call, 59, 76–77
cruising: coastal cruising applications of ham radio, 72–73; Coastal 2 mobile repeating stations, 105–7; licenses recommendations, 20–21; open water cruising applications of ham radio, 76–77; popular bands, 69

daytime and nighttime wave propagation, 67–71
DC ground, 40
DC power, 38
DFing, 27–28
digital data (computer), 15
direction finding, 27–28
distance transmission (DX) contests, 14. *See also* awards; contests
distress frequencies, 65, 67, 68
down switch, 55
DXCC (DX Century Club) award, 22. *See also* awards; contests

earth-moon-earth contacts (EME), 25
80-meter band, 68–69
80-meter band propagation conditions, 68–69
electromagnetic frequency spectrum, 62
e-mail: about, 77; access, 77–81, 82; capability, 3, 21, 29, 82; address, 77, 81; computer and operating system requirements, 78; modem, 78–79; radio equipment, 78; requirements, 78; setup and adapters, **80–81**; software, 79–80; weather forecasts, 82–83; Winlink 2000 System, 79–81
EME operation, 25
emergency distress frequencies, 65, 67, 68

119

United States Power Squadrons is all about boating education, safety, and enjoyment

United States Power Squadrons (USPS) is a private organization with 50,000 enthusiastic members interested in all types of boating—motoring, sailing, paddling, rowing, fishing, cruising, hunting, and water sports—in 450 squadrons in the United States, Puerto Rico, and Japan.

USPS is all about education and sharing boating experiences. Through our courses, books, guides, presentations, and seminars, we've been teaching safe boating since 1914. USPS members include experts from the boating world: authors of leading marine books, magazine articles, and guides; USCG licensed masters and captains; and participants of many boards and commissions on marine topics worldwide. USPS members and the public enjoy courses created and taught by our volunteer instructors, at very reasonable costs. Courses and seminars include:

- Basic Boating
- Seamanship
- GPS
- Coastal and Inland Navigation
- Understanding and Using Charts
- Offshore Navigation
- Celestial Navigation
- Marine Weather
- Marine Electronics
- Marine Engine Maintenance
- Cruise Planning
- Sailing
- Instructor Development and Certification

Members place a high value on fellowship through social events and civic service. Our members actively participate in the boating community through education, vessel safety checks, and a cooperative program with the National Oceanic and Atmospheric Administration (NOAA) to update navigation charts. USPS even maintains a network of port captains who provide expert local information for visiting boaters.

Perhaps the greatest benefit of participation with the United States Power Squadrons is the enjoyment, camaraderie, and opportunity to share experiences and ideas with other members, and to help the boating public. United States Power Squadrons endeavors to make boating a safer, more enjoyable experience for everyone. To learn more, visit www.usps.org.

Look for these other USPS Guides:

The Boatowner's Guide to GMDSS and Marine Radio
Celestial Sight Reduction Methods
Compass Installation and Adjusting
Knots, Bends, and Hitches for Mariners
Radar and GPS
Skipper Saver